JAYAN E. ROMESH

C-O-M-P-A-S-S-I-O-N

Secrets and Science of Compassionate Living

A Metta Library Publication

Copyright © 2020 by

Jayan Romesh Edirisinghe

All rights reserved. No part of this book may be reproduced in any manner without the prior written permission of the author.

Published 2020

Book designed by Jayan E. Romesh

ISBN : 9798635030271

BOOKS
FOR A CAUSE

This Book is Dedicated to All Compassionate People

Acknowledgements

I would like to acknowledge each of my loving and compassionate thoughts, circumstances, and the wise people who have led me to embrace the world with compassion. I want to acknowledge anyone who will learn the teachings in this message and open your heart and deepen your understanding wherever you are.

I am grateful for all the spiritual teachers who live the message of these emotions.

It is with deep gratitude that I acknowledge and thank Dr. Rick Hanson, Professor Linda Christensen, Dr. Suman Kollipara, all my spiritual teachers - Adrianne Ross, Rachel Lewis, and Karen Lawrie at British Columbia Insight Meditation Society, Michele McDonald, and Jesse Maceo Vega-Frey from Insight Meditation society, Barre, Massachusetts, Marian Smith and Brett at Mindful Living, Vancouver, all my loving friends for their wisdom, insights, teachings, and encouragements.

I am also grateful for all who gave me loving support and harmonious efforts to transform the manuscript into this book and bring it out into the world.

Finally, I would like to express my loving kindness and gratitude to my mother Charitha Edirisinghe, my wife Manjula P. Edirisinghe, my mother in-law Leticia Rajapaksa, and all family members, friends, and readers without whom this book would not have come into existence. To my spiritual friends, and to the greatest teacher in the world, this precious life on Planet Earth.

It is my humble aspiration that you find this book helpful and that it provides you with clear, practical wisdom, and tools for your happiness, well-being and compassionate life.

May the merits from this gift of Wisdom bless my late loving father Don Francis Edirisinghe and my late loving father in-law R.R.W Rajapaksa.

*"May all beings be free from suffering
and causes of suffering."*

Author Foreword

This book is about a new sense of awareness and understanding through compassion. It is opening your heart to boundless qualities to embrace the world with compassion.

Compassion is known as the quivering of the heart in response to pain or suffering. Pain and suffering is a tremendously powerful teacher and an opening. We can blame ourselves for seemingly being ineffectual in a world that needs so much help.

Compassion allows us to use our own pain and the pain of others as a vehicle for understanding and connection. This is a profound practice. We may be averse to seeing our own suffering because it tends to ignite a blaze of self-blame and regret. And we may be averse to seeing suffering in others because we find it unbearable or we find it threatening to our own happiness. All of these possible reactions to the suffering in the world makes us want to turn away from life.

In contrast, compassion manifests in us as the offering of kindness rather than withdrawal. Because compassion is a state of mind that is itself open, abundant, and inclusive, it allows us to meet pain and suffering more directly. With direct seeing, we know that we are not alone in our suffering and that no one need feel alone when in pain. Seeing our interconnectedness is the beginning of our compassion and it allows us to reach beyond aversion and separation.

The stability of the heart of compassion comes from wisdom of clear seeing. We don't have to struggle to be someone we are not, hating ourselves for our fears or our guilt. One of the things that most nourishes true compassion is clarity, and right understanding. The Buddha said at one point that if we truly loved ourselves we would never harm another, because if we harm another it is in some way diminishing who we are, it is taking away from rather than adding to our lives.

Compassion is like a mirror into which we can always look. It is like a stream that steadily carries us, It is like a cleansing fire that continually transforms us. Compassion is about being more and more compassionate towards ourselves and towards others. It is not about assuming a new self-image or manufactured persona; it is about being compassionate naturally out of what we see, out of what we understand. My right effort is to bring you that understanding, through reflections, meditations, and practices in this life transforming guide.

These boundless practices are extended to all beings, and in the sense that they can be applied to all situations where they are appropriate. You can feel compassion for all who are suffering, regardless of what they did to bring on that suffering.

In practice, people will find true happiness only if they understand the causes of compassion and act on them.

*"Let no one deceive another
Or despise anyone anywhere,
Or through anger or resistance,
Wish for another to suffer."*

Compassion is what grows out of boundless love when you see suffering. You want the suffering to stop.

When you encounter suffering that you can't stop no matter how hard you try, you need a peaceful state of mind to avoid creating additional suffering. It simply makes kindness more focused and effective by opening your boundless heart to the lessons of your wise mind. This book will illuminate the boundless qualities of heart and mind, leading to a happiness that is lasting and true. The cultivation of these qualities will pave the way for compassion.

We can learn to practice compassion in everyday situations. The more mindful you are, the more you see that our lives are really interconnected. We have a connection by just being here, sharing this life and this planet. The more clearly you see this, the less hatred and suffering there will be in your mind and you will embrace the world with compassion.

Jayan E. Romesh
Vancouver, BC

*"May I mindfully meet
The suffering of others
With an open heart,
compassionately sharing with them
the emotions
natural to our human condition."*

Birth of Compassion

"Compassion is about developing genuine concern for others with sympathy, feelings of closeness, and a sense of responsibility."

In the year of 2010, lifestyle changes created a shift in my life. With mindfulness I started to noticed subtle changes. I was more patient with others and was less reactive, more open, more aware, and more in control of my life. I was living through the challenge of radiating compassion. Whatever I did deepened my path with mindfulness and compassionate qualities.

When we look around, we see joy and sadness, we see suffering and delight, we see a longing to be touched, and a fear of being touched all together. We see a longing to be free and a fear of being free, side by side. And in ourselves, we see the same. We are all the same. Each one of us is complete and contains the whole universe. And each one of us is caught in the delusion of being separate. Sometimes we forget our way from time to time and fall back into the habit of clinging to the old separate self. And each time we do, suffering occurs. The process of waking up to mindfulness needs continuous renewal, just as each breath we take nourishes us and keeps us alive. We can't wake up once and stay awake to the amazing interconnectedness of everything without continuous effort.

All life is interrelated. We are made to live together because of the interrelated structure of reality. We are all caught in an inescapable network of life tied into a common destiny.

If our actions are infused with a vision of interconnectedness, then love, kindness, and compassion will keep us going in our efforts. It is a direct seeing of a deeper reality. What happens in one place is consequential elsewhere, precisely because we are interconnected. The law of interconnectedness asks us to let go of rigid differences, to be responsive to the needs of others, to know that by taking care of others we are taking care of ourselves. The fact that everyone and everything has an effect on their surroundings is a call to honor our interconnection and show compassion towards all other beings. Respecting this interconnection can open us to an honest and mindful life with compassion. We cannot avert our eyes, looking around at those who suffer, are hungry, are ill, or frightened. Our picture of life necessarily includes concern for everybody and the environment. Environmental awareness shows us that there is no us and them. What happens over there does indeed have an effect on what happens to us over here.

There are times when we can be cut off from reality. We need to take the time to have an understanding of the layers of conditions coming together for even one meal: the people growing our food, the animals giving up their milk, the planet nurturing us all. The clarity of perception is the root of understanding and the birth of compassion.

Hearts of Compassion

"Compassion opens the willingness to observe negative thoughts and emotions with openness and clarity."

Any seeming mistake can provoke self-blame, shame, kindness, or compassion. Any trait we see in ourselves or others, emotional storm, or experience of life's difficulties can be responded to in many different ways. One response we can consciously cultivate is compassion and self-compassion. Compassion and self-compassion involve recognizing the suffering of others and ourselves. Compassion allows us to use our own pain and the pain of others as a vehicle for connection. It opens the willingness to observe negative thoughts and emotions with openness and clarity, so that they are held in mindful awareness. Mindfulness is a non-judgmental, receptive state of mind in which one observes thoughts and feelings as they are, without trying to suppress or deny them. We cannot ignore pain and feel compassion for it at the same time. The development of compassion, through the cultivation of mindful awareness and loving kindness, is a way we can come up against life's inevitable frustrations, mistakes, and disappointments. As an ability, love is always there as a potential, ready to flourish and help our lives flourish. As we go up and down in life, as we acquire or lose, as we are showered with praise or unfairly blamed, always within there is the ability of love with equanimity. Life is so fragile, with its shifts from pleasure to pain, from ease to difficult confrontations, and from getting what we want to watching what we just got begin to fade away. Remember that even people who have more than us suffer. Rejoice in the happiness of others. Love everything unconditionally. Open your heart to the suffering of others with compassion. Connect fully to whatever is happening around you without rushing towards what is pleasant and pulling away from what is unpleasant, stilling the mind with equanimity, love the whole world with universal love and awaken to your precious and miraculous life on Earth.

Widening the Circle of Compassion

*"May I mindfully meet
the suffering of others
with an open heart,
compassionately sharing with them
the emotions
natural to our human condition."*

The clarity of perception is the root of understanding and the birth of compassion. Compassion is a quivering of the heart that arises in response to suffering. If loving kindness embodies the wish for all beings to be happy under all conditions, then compassion is what happens when this goodwill encounters suffering – the heart wishes for the alleviation of suffering. Compassion manifests as non-cruelty, and its proximate cause is seeing the pain and helplessness in those disadvantaged or overtaken by some misfortune.

The far enemy of compassion is cruelty and compassion succeeds when it makes such feelings subside. Compassion fails when it causes sorrow. When faced with suffering, if one is overwhelmed by grief or heaviness of heart, then that is not being compassionate. When one is drawn towards boundlessness, it is not dragged down by suffering. Instead, it is uplifted. If one's mind is affected by grief, then one is not able to respond in a clear and open-hearted manner. This is why sorrow and grief are characterized as the near enemy of compassion. Both responses can spring from seeing suffering in others, but grief has a depressive effect, while compassion has a positive and uplifting quality.

The far enemy of compassion is cruelty or the wish for harm. The near enemy of compassion is a sense of being overwhelmed, of feeling the suffering with the other person so intensely that one is in too much pain to be of much use. Without the buoyancy that goodwill gives us, it is possible to drown in another's suffering.

As with goodwill, we start the practice of compassion by offering compassion to ourselves. It is difficult to bear witness to the suffering of others. We can invite compassion for ourselves because we have our own suffering. When we do this, we are more available to be present for the suffering of others. If your compassion does not include yourself, it is incomplete. Compassion invites us to have less separation between our suffering and that of others, while giving us something strong to hold on to, widening the circle of compassion.

Beyond Suffering

"Only the person involved in self-investigation can be aware of the causes of this suffering and know the path leading to overcome the suffering."

Someone who cultivates compassion becomes sensitive to the suffering they create for themselves and for others. They are qualities that develop the heart, and mind by cultivating compassion and abiding in it, bringing happiness to others and to oneself. As your heart becomes sensitive and open, you realize that suffering is painful and do not want to abide in it.

Only the person involved in self-investigation can be aware of the causes of this suffering and know the path leading to overcome the suffering. Buddha's Four Noble Truths is the fruit of this methodical self-inquiry, which was practiced for centuries. The Four Noble Truths are the basic principles of a practical manual for understanding the alleviating human suffering, which can be viewed not as dogmas, but more as four working hypotheses for life that can be repeatedly tested by means of our own experience. They are the ancient teachings based on compassion to elevate human suffering.

In the modern scientific world, many manuals have been developed as a response to human suffering, in medicine as well as in clinical psychology.

> *"Recognizing that everything in life is impermanent, may we recall the universality of suffering and gain understanding to the Noble Truths of reality."*

Four Noble Truths

"Just like a physician, the Buddha made a diagnosis, analyzed the cause, offered a prognosis and proposed a therapy. He called for careful investigation of the processes in our own mind and body, advising people not just to believe him but to investigate everything for themselves."

"It is through not understanding, not realizing four things, that I, disciples, as well as you, had to wander so long through this round of rebirths. And what are these four things. They are,

The noble truth of suffering,

The noble truth of the origin of suffering,

The noble truth of the extinction of suffering,

The noble truth of the path that leads to the extinction of suffering."

-The Buddha

The Truth

The First Noble Truth is the simple acknowledgement (diagnosis) that suffering is an inevitable part of existence. There is suffering. Just consider the universal phenomena of illness, aging, and death. And apart from these are of course many forms of inevitable suffering, like not being able to get what we want, being confronted with unwanted situations, being separated from what is dear to us, or experiencing unpleasant emotions and thoughts. Our lives often do not run smoothly. There may be many moments of happiness, but we cannot hold on to them. Inherent to human life is a fundamental state of dissatisfaction or dis-ease. The First Noble Truth acknowledges this fundamental fact explaining the following eleven types of suffering.

Eleven types of Sufferings:

1. Birth
2. Decay
3. Death
4. Sorrow
5. Lamentation
6. Bodily ill
7. Mental ill
8. Ill of despair
9. Ill due to association with enemies
10. Ill due to separation from loved ones
11. Ill due to non-fulfilment of wishes

"The truth that all sentient life involves suffering. This is so because all sentient existence bears the three characteristics of impermanence, unsatisfactoriness, and the absence of any real, enduring ego-entity."

The Cause

The Second Noble Truth – there is a cause of suffering – unveils that cause. It involves three phenomena that are called the three poisons in the Buddha's teachings. They are greed, aversion, and delusion. Whenever we are overpowered by desire for experiences that are impermanent by nature, this causes suffering. When we are overpowered by aversion to pain or unpleasant experiences that are inevitable, this adds more suffering. When it is not possible to see reality clearly because we are blinded by judgments and fixed opinions, this can lead to much suffering. It involves understanding mental phenomena that can be investigated here and now in our consciousness by mindfulness. If these causes remain unconscious, they constantly condition our actions and keep us imprisoned in our suffering. If we practice mindfulness regularly, we learn from our own experience which processes reinforces suffering and which alleviate it.

"The five aggregates- material form, feelings, perceptions, mental formations and consciousness are a classificatory scheme for understanding the nature of our being. We are the five and the five are us. Whatever we identify with, whatever we hold to as our self, falls within the set of five aggregates. Why should the Buddha say that the five aggregates are suffering. The reason Buddha says that the five aggregates are suffering is that they are impermanent. They change from moment to moment, arise and fall away. There nothing we can cling to in them as a basis for security. There is only a constantly disintergrating flux which, when clung to in the desire for permanence, brings a plunge into suffering like touching fire causes harm."

The Liberation

The Third Noble Truth offers a prognosis, namely that liberation or inner freedom from suffering is possible. Through awareness and insight into suffering as a result of greed, aversion, and ignorance, we can wake up or awaken to a state of more inner freedom. When we see our conditioning, space arises for other possibilities. Acknowledging and accepting the processes as they naturally occur without clinging or aversion towards them favourably affects the prognosis. The word Buddha means awakened. Awakened to what? Awakened to the nature of existence. We all have the potential to awaken understanding the– suffering, impermanence, and non-self – nature of existence.

The Path

The Fourth Noble Truth prescribes the Eightfold Path (the treatment) as a way to liberation from suffering. This is a path of practice and self-inquiry that everyone can follow. The Noble Eightfold Path involves cultivating insight (right view, right intention), ethics (right speech, right action, and right livelihood) and meditation (right effort, right mindfulness, and right concentration). We need to discover for ourselves what is wholesome, skillful or beneficial by testing it against our own experience. The various stages of this Noble Eightfold Path of practice are not independent from each other. Practicing one aspect reinforces the other aspects; neglecting one part will have an effect on the others.

The Four Noble Truths encourages an attitude of care.

Noble Eightfold Path in a Nutshell

1. Right View: insight into the true nature of reality by understanding the Four Noble Truths. Cultivating perspectives that enable us to see through delusion and discern the true nature of reality.
2. Right Intention: cultivating renunciation, good will, and harmlessness or compassion.
3. Right Speech: using speech compassionately.
4. Right Action: ethical conduct, manifesting compassion. Act for the greater good without causing harm.
5. Right Livelihood: making a living through ethical and non - harmful means.
6. Right Effort: cultivating wholesome qualities, releasing unwholesome qualities.
7. Right Mindfulness: whole body and mind awareness. Observe and become

familiar with the mind, distinguishing between raw sensory input and mental phenomena in response to sensory input, such as feelings, emotions, thoughts, mind states, and interpretations.

8. Right Concentration: through meditation practice, seeing deeply into the nature of reality with stability of mind.

*"Commit not
to harm others
through thoughts, words, and deeds
inspire to work
to bring a compassionate world."*

Liberation from Suffering

There are three antidotes that are effective against the three poisons of greed, hatred, and delusion, that creates suffering. All three of these can be cultivated by the practice of the Noble Eightfold Path: generosity, or not being attached to what is impermanent; compassion, or facing pain with care and concern; and insight into the fact that all phenomena are ultimately impermanent, unsatisfactory and uncontrollable. Insight into our selfless nature is part of this too because our ego or self and everything we identify with just as temporary and impermanent as all other phenomena. Getting attached to what is fleeting is what creates dis-ease and suffering.

The liberating processes of ancient psychology shows similarities with the techniques of behavior therapy. The cognitive therapy of the second generation chose to work in the area of correcting dysfunctional thoughts and beliefs – cognitive restructuring – by inviting patients to view themselves and the world from healthier cognitions and to act accordingly.

Mindfulness based exercises are taught to defuse or dis-identify from views about ourselves, the world, the past, and the future with which we are fused or overidentified. Defusion of our self-image opens up our awareness and shifts the perspective from self-as-content to self-as-context, the empty space that the stream of experiences flows through and is somewhat similar to the Buddha's teaching of selflessness. Thus our consciousness becomes a constantly available holding environment with unconditional space and acceptance for all our experiences, pleasant and unpleasant.

Fusion and experiential avoidance are processes that prolong our suffering in the wheel of existence and prevent us from aligning our lives with our values, with what really matters. Defusion and acceptance pave the way for a life where we are committed to our values. Self-inquiry into our inner world, where we can find the causes for our suffering as well as the keys to free ourselves from it leads to practice mindfulness based compassionate living. With mindfulness practices, we bring our attention again to the experience of the present moment, so that we can learn to make the distinction between wholesome or unwholesome reactions to suffering and learn to trust the secure holding of being tenderly and mindfully present with whatever is happening. Mindfulness becomes heartfulness. The effects of practice of compassion and goodwill are increasingly being studied. While mindfulness trainings help us to open our eyes so that what appears to us from moment to moment can be seen clearly, compassion training can help to open the heart to what is being seen, particularly when it is painful and unpleasant. Deeper levels of goodwill and compassion can be a healing force, even if all else fails.

Opening the Heart

"May all living beings be free from suffering and the causes of suffering."

There is this inner understanding in each of us. Each of us has an amazing noble character that cannot be destroyed by suffering or taken away by force. It is the source of true happiness and contentment. The way we develop this inner, noble character is through compassion. Compassion is an experience that allows us to feel our interconnectedness. We all share some of the same circumstances in life. This helps us loose our self-illusion. Much of our suffering comes from being too immersed in our self-illusion. Compassion is the best way to cure this illness, the illness of loneliness, isolation, and alienation. Compassion is a beautiful bridge between ourselves and others. Compassion is defined as the very authentic emotion that we want every living being to be free from suffering. We can embrace the world with compassion, as we do in the following practice.

Compassion Meditation

Sit down in a comfortable posture in a quiet place - a shrine room, a quiet room, a park, or any other place providing privacy and silence. Keeping the eyes closed, repeat the word compassion a few times and mentally visualize its significance - boundless compassion as the opposite of suffering and causes of suffering, and as a profound feeling of boundlessness.

Now visualize your own face in a happy and radiant mood. Having visualized yourself in a happy frame of mind, first begin by sending compassion to yourself, which opens our hearts to others.

Use the following phrases:

"May I be free from suffering and causes of suffering."

Keep feeling that boundless compassion. Sense that loving wishes flowing through your heart, perhaps in a rhythm with the breath. Feel how that compassionate energy, flowing through your heart, is not specific to any one person.

After directing compassion to yourself, you move on to someone you find inspiring, or to whom you feel grateful and who are also living- monks, teachers, parents, and elders. Bring the person's presence into your mind and direct the loving phrases toward him or her:

"May you be free from suffering and causes of suffering."

Next, one should visualize neutral people, people for whom one has neither like nor dislike, such as one's neighbours, colleagues, and so on and radiate boundless compassion to them.

Having radiated compassionate thoughts to everyone in the neutral circle, one should now visualize persons for whom one has dislike, hostility or prejudice, even whom one may have had a temporary misunderstanding.

As one visualizes disliked persons, to each one, you must mentally repeat: "I have no hostility toward him/ her, may he/ she also not have any hostility towards me. May he/ she be free from suffering and causes of suffering."

Thus, as one visualizes the persons of the different circles, one breaks the barrier caused by likes and dislikes, attachment and hatred. When one is able to regard an enemy without ill-will and with the same amount of goodwill that one has for a very dear friend, goodwill then acquires a boundless, sublime impartiality, elevating the mind upward and outward as if in a spiral movement of ever-widening circle of compassion until it becomes all-embracing.

A goodwill-thought is a powerful thought-force. It can actually effect what has been willed. For wishing well-being is willing and thus is creative action. Radiation of thought of compassion, too, is the development of a willpower that can effect whatever is willed. It is not a rare experience to see diseases cured or misfortunes warded off- even from a great distance, by the application of the thought-force of boundless goodwill.

In the final phase, we offer compassion to all beings everywhere. This method can present an impersonal mode of radiating compassion, which makes the mind truly all-embracing. This is the way to the liberation of mind through boundless compassion. The unliberated mind is imprisoned within the walls of egocentricity, greed, hatred, delusion, jealousy, and meanness. As long as the mind is in the grip of these defiling and limiting mental factors, for so long it remains fettered. By breaking these bonds, compassion liberates the mind, and the liberated mind naturally grows boundless and immeasurable.

Imagine the people residing in your house and then embrace all of them within your heart, radiating the compassionate thoughts. Having visualized one's own house in this manner, one must now visualize the next house, and all its residents, and then the next house, and the next, and so on, until all the houses in that street are similarly covered by all-embracing boundless compassionate energy.

Now the meditator should take up the next street, and the next, until the entire neighbourhood or village is covered. Thereafter extension by extension, direction wise, should be clearly visualized and spread with compassionate-rays in abundant measure. In this way, the entire town or the city to be covered; then the district and entire state should be covered and radiated with thoughts of compassion.

Next, one should visualize state after state, starting with one's own state, then the rest of the states in the different directions, the east, south, west, and north. Thus one should cover the whole of one's country, regardless of class, race, sect or religion. Think:

"May everyone in this great land abide in peace and well-being. May there be no war, no strife, no misfortune, and no maladies. Radiant with friendliness and good fortune, with compassion and wisdom, may all those in this great country enjoy peace and plenty."

One should now cover the entire continent, country by country in the eastern, southern, western, and northern directions. Geographically imagining each country and the people therein according to their looks, one should radiate in abundant measure thoughts of compassion:

"May they be free from suffering and causes of suffering."

Thereafter one should take up all the continents - Africa, Asia, Australia, Europe, North, and South America- visualizing country by country and people by people, covering the entire globe. Imagine yourself at a particular point of the globe and then project powerful rays of goodwill, enveloping one direction of the globe, then another, then another and so on until the whole globe is flooded and thoroughly enveloped with glowing thoughts of compassion.

One should now project into the vastness of space powerful beams of compassion towards all beings living in other realms, first in the four cardinal directions- east, south, west and north- then in the intermediary directions-northeast, southeast, southwest, northwest- and then above and below, coverings all the ten directions with abundant and measureless thoughts of compassion.

You may sense this boundless compassion like a warmth or light. Or like a spreading pool, with gentle waves extending farther and farther to include all beings.

Take a few minutes to explore extending your boundless compassion to all-beings living on earth and beyond. Your universal compassion is extending to all living beings on this earth and embracing the world with compassion.

"May all beings be free from suffering and causes of suffering."

The radiation in this case becomes a flowing out of boundless compassion in abundant measure towards all beings, all creatures, etc. seen and unseen.

When one projects this total wish for others to dwell happily, free from hostility, affliction and distress, not only does one elevate oneself to a level where true happiness prevails, but one sets in motion powerful vibrations conducing to happiness, cooling off enmity, relieving affliction and distress. Boundless and universal compassion brings well-being and happiness and removes the mental and physical suffering caused by the mental pollutants of hostility, enmity and anger.

Micro Compassion Meditation

"May you be free from suffering and causes of suffering."

Goodwill of Compassion

"As we go up and down in life, as we acquire or lose, as we are showered with praise or unfairly blamed, always within there is the ability of compassion with equanimity."

Compassion in Action

In your day-to-day life, when you find yourself suffering or are in the presence of suffering, you might try breathing in the feeling of compassion for yourself by imagining carrying in a kind word or a sense of warmth on the inhale, and then breathing out compassion on the exhale.

Consider a situation in the world or in your own life that might be improved by compassion. Imagine how the situation could be different if the people involved in it felt, thought, and acted with compassion, wishing others not to suffer.

"May you be free of your pain and sorrow."

"May you find peace."

Glimpse of Compassion

Beyond attending to a suffering person, another access to the practice involves attending to someone who is engaged in very harmful actions - actions dominated by malice, self-centeredness, greed, jealousy, or cruelty.

Bring this person vividly to the mind. What is it that makes this person appear so vile? It could be his behavior, disposition, and certain mental traits. Then, briefly bring your awareness back to yourself and imagine what it would be like if you yourself were afflicted with a similar disposition, similar habits of behavior. You may sense your horizons shutting down, your world growing smaller, your heart becoming contorted. You may sense the pain and anxiety that ensue from such affliction. Yearn to be free of these afflictions of the mind. Restore yourself to the light and imagine being utterly free of them. Once again, sense the spaciousness, the lightness, the buoyancy, the soothing calm of freedom from those afflictions.

Turn your awareness back to the same person, and say, "just as I wish to be free of such afflictions and harmful behavior, may you also be free." Look to the person who is afflicted, without equating the person with the temporary afflictions of personality and behavior patterns. Look at the person, who like yourself, simply yearns for happiness, and wishes to be free of suffering. Let your own desires fuse with those of this person.

"May you indeed be free of suffering. May you find the rich happiness and well-being that you seek. May all the sources of unhappiness and conflict fall away. May you be free of suffering and its sources."

Like the sun appearing through a break in the clouds, like a blossom bursting forth from dark soil, imagine this person emerging from the suffering and from the source of suffering. Imagine this person as vividly as you can, free of those sources of suffering. Now expand the scope of this compassion to all sentient beings in each of the four corners, attending first to the reality that each one essentially wishes to be free of suffering. It is this yearning that accounts for such diverse behavior. Let your heart be joined with the essential yearning.

"May you indeed be free of suffering, just as I myself wish to be free of suffering."

Let your body fill with light and send it out to each of the four quarters. Imagine sentient beings in each of these regions emerging from suffering and the source of suffering.

"If you want to be happy, practice compassion."

"The compassion of the wise man does not render him a victim of suffering. His thoughts, words, and deeds are full of pity. But his heart does not waver; unchanged it remains, serene and calm. Compassion is a beautiful quality of the heart and intellect which knows, understands and is ready to help. Compassion that is strength and gives strength: this is the highest compassion. The highest manifestation of compassion is to show the world the path leading to the end of suffering."

"We cannot avert our eyes, looking around at those who suffer, those who are hungry, those who are ill or frightened. Our picture of life necessarily includes concern for everybody and everything including the environment."

None of us can live alone. We are all dependent on each other. What do we need to learn in order to live together as brothers and sisters? The answer is compassion.

The world suffers with its ever increasing business; the result of an attachment to impermanence and delusion. We do not notice the stranger in front of us. There are more urgent things to pay attention to moment to moment, like the text message on our phones. The fact is, whether it's yourself in the mirror, a loved one, or a stranger, you miss noticing the uniqueness and the needs of the human being in front of you. What would it be like to set the right intention and give some mindful attention to the world in need around you with compassion? It will open you in beautiful ways. Mindfulness facilitates the experience of connection with ourselves and with others. It is an experience of coming home to oneness and fullness.

"Most men have their eyes and ears closed to the suffering of others. They do not hear the cries of distress. They become deaf to their pleas and blind to their plight. They do not see the unbroken stream of tears flowing through life; they do not hear the cries of distress continually pervading the world. Bound by selfishness, their hearts turn stiff and narrow. Stiff and narrow, how should they be able to strive for any higher purpose? To realize, that only the release of selfish cravings will affect their own freedom from suffering."

Only by transcending the ego, relinquishment of self, and by understanding reality, can we release ourselves from our prison, and having done so will we be able to help others end their suffering. When wisdom is present with the right view, there is compassionate action. The natural response of one who is free from defilement is compassion. As the mind gets clearer, the heart is less burdened with attachments and defilements, and one is able to respond with compassion. Compassion opens the heart, takes the blindfold off our eyes, and opens our ears to the reality of a profoundly suffering world.

It is compassion that removes the obstacles and opens the door to freedom, making the narrow heart as wide as the world. Compassion reconciles us with our own destiny by showing us the life of others, often much harder than ours. Open your heart to glowing compassion.

Feeling compassion means being concerned about the suffering of others and wishing them to be free of suffering and its causes. Compassion is closely related to loving kindness, which is the wish for living beings to have happiness and its causes.

If we don't care for others, all of us will suffer. Compassion applies to all areas of our lives: on a personal level, compassion for ourselves, for friends and family, for our colleagues and our boss, and even for the people who sometimes disturb us; on a community level, compassion of one group and the other group; on an international level, compassion of one nation and for the citizens of other nations.

Compassion is the opposite of our self-centeredness that urges us to get the best and most for ourselves in order to ensure our own happiness. Self-centeredness results in difficulties for those around us, and their problems disturb not only their tranquility but ours as well.

"Although we may win arguments, when we care only for ourselves, when we humiliate people and ignore their misery, it will almost always come back to us through the "Law of Karma." Therefore, if we want to be happy, it is essential to care for the welfare of others rather than categorizing some people as "enemies" whose needs are not important. We can instead care for their well-being. When we respect them as human beings, help them meet their basic needs and their need to be respected, to give and receive care and affection, and to contribute to the welfare of a group, there will be no reason for them to be enemies. An enemy will become a friend."

Human beings are more dependent on each other now than any other time in human existence. Many of us do not know how we depend on each other, as well as on those who make the roads we drive on, who invent the technology we use, and who teaches us everything we know. Once we recognize our interconnectedness, the law of interconnectedness asks us to let go of rigid differences, to be responsive to the needs of others, to know that by taking care of others we are taking care of ourselves. The fact that everyone and everything has an effect on their surroundings is a call to honor our interconnection and show compassion towards all other beings. Respecting this interconnection can open us to an honest and mindful life with compassion. With compassion, we respect their choices, and we are ready to help them help themselves, if they ask for it.

"Environmental awareness and threats of diseases shows us that there is no "us" and "them." What happens "over there" does indeed have an effect on what happens to us "over here." We see that caring for each other is more crucial than ever before. We have exceptional human brains, something no other species has, so we have to use our intelligence to help each other. Then, all of us will benefit and live together peacefully. Compassion is the way to do this."

"The foundation of compassion is when you come to perceive the real causes of suffering; an attachment to impermanence, delusional beliefs about the world, and selfish habits. When we see selfish, deluded people, we know that suffering is never far away. When we transcend our own self-centeredness and perceive the truth, compassion naturally follows."

As you go through your day and encounter different people, remind yourself that like you, one of their deepest, innermost wishes is to be happy and not suffer. When you experience your daily activities, look at the people around you and reflect,

"This person, like me, wants to be happy and avoid suffering. "Let this knowledge enter your heart."

Then take it a step further and extend a kind wish to them,

"May you be happy and free from suffering."

Similarly we can extend this kind wish to ourselves. Repeatedly extending compassionate wishes can transform our minds, as we gradually build compassionate habits, they replace our habits to judge, criticize and shame that keeps us caught up in anger, anxiety and negativity.

Mindful Reflection

With the intention to cultivate positive qualities, you can contribute to the happiness of everyone with whom you come into contact, including yourself. Imagine acting with the sincere motivation to make the world around you a kinder, happier place and to reduce the suffering of those you interact with, embracing with compassion. Try taking a moment to set your motivation each morning before getting out of bed:

"Today I will do my best to show kindness and compassion to those with whom I interact." "Today I will try to be less judgmental." "Today, I will provide a model of patience and perseverance to serve others."

Experiment with setting your motivation in this way each morning and see how this impacts your day.

Mindful Way to Compassion

"If we are not paying attention, we can lose ourselves in destructive thoughts and emotions, and our compassion quickly fades away."

A common obstacle to cultivate compassion occurs when our minds are swept away by troublesome emotions or thoughts. it is relatively easy to experience kindness and compassion when everything is going well. The trouble comes when anger, fear, jealousy, anxiety, critical thoughts, and so on leap into our minds. If we are not paying attention, we can lose ourselves in such thoughts and emotions, and our compassion quickly fades away.

Over the last few decades, western mental health professionals have used mindfulness based approaches adapted from ancient teachings to help their patients work with difficult thoughts and emotions. A quickly growing body of research shows that the regular practice of mindfulness meditation can even lead to growth in areas of the brain linked with emotion regulation, sense of self-identity, compassion and empathy.

Mindfulness is generally defined as purposeful, non-judgmental awareness of what is happening inside of us and around us in the present moment. With mindful awareness, we neither cling to nor reject our experiences; we simply notice and accept them as they are. For example, we can discuss a sensitive issue with a family member and notice our voice is growing louder with an edge to it. We can become aware that this is because we feel threatened and are getting defensive and angry. This mindful awareness gives us the ability to make wise choices – for example, to slow down and to think before we speak. If we fail to notice troublesome thoughts and emotions and to recognize them as temporary mental experiences, it can be easy to be swept away by them.

Mindful awareness can help us notice when we are overcome by powerful emotions, so we steer ourselves towards a better course of action. "I am really angry right now. Anything I say to him, while I am feeling this way is likely to be hurtful, so I will better keep quiet for the time being."

Having taken a step back from the powerful emotion, a host of other possibilities open up, like slowing down breathing, reminding the real nature of the situation. Once you calm down, you might even become aware of this as a valuable teaching experience - a chance for transformation.

With mindfulness, we train ourselves to recognize and accept our mental experiences as temporary mental experiences, without judging or clinging to them. Relating to our thoughts and emotions as temporary experiences rather than identifying them as who we are or as the way things are gives us some space to work with them. It is the difference between getting completely caught up in anger and instead observing, the emotional state of anger.

"Mindfulness is generally defined as purposeful, non-judgmental awareness of what is happening inside of us and around us in the present moment."

RAIN

Recognize – Allow – Investigate – No Identification

RAIN is an acronym based meditation process based on bare attention. It is the best of this kind of acronym meditation by far and so many people have found it to be a lifesaver when it all gets a bit too much.

The way it works is by you simply going through each of the four stages in turn and in doing so, you will find some space from that which feels too much to bear.

The acronym RAIN can be useful in helping us to remember the psychological process involved in mindfulness:

The first stage is **Recognize**. That is bare awareness, recognizing what it is that's happening, not what you think is happening.

The next stage is **Allow**. Even though it is hard, is there something in you that can just let what is happening happen.

The third stage is **Investigate**. What else can you discover about the experience? Are there any more details to notice or any other sensations happening at the same time?

The final stage is No-**Identification**. Are you able to see that by observing the difficulty, it is not a part of you?

Those are the four stages of RAIN.

Mindfulness allows us to have an accepting, nonjudgmental awareness of our thoughts and emotions, without necessarily buying into them. This changes how we think and talk about our emotions, for example recognizing that I am feeling anger, rather than I am angry. The first statement recognizes anger as an experience within awareness, a temporary mental state. The second reflects identification; we feel fused with the emotion and can't see a way to work with it.

Mindfulness helps us develop compassion because the more aware we are of our shifting thoughts and emotional states, the better prepared we will be to work with the difficult ones and to cultivate the mental experiences that we want to have like compassion with right effort and mindfulness. In this way, we practice mindfulness and compassion in tandem. Thinking, *"I am feeling anxious, angry, jealous, sad right now. How can I help myself work with this suffering?"*

A common method of training in mindfulness begins with mindfully observing the breath. As we practice mindful breathing, we don't automatically get caught up in unproductive thoughts and emotions that make us miserable. The purpose of returning our attention to the breath whenever it gets distracted is not to suppress or ignore our destructing thoughts and emotions; it is to help us learn to notice them and to give us some mental space so we don't automatically get caught up in them.

Awakening Mindfulness of Breath

The miracle of breath that connects life to consciousness

This exercise develops our awareness of breathing in and out. Our breath is the bridge from our body to our mind. Take a few deep and moderately forceful breaths and then flow into your natural rhythm of respiration. This is a practice of simply watching the breath and being with the breath. By doing this practice, we are letting ourselves experience the process of how breathing changes in the body. Let the breath come and go. See for yourself that sometimes it is short or shallow, sometimes deep, sometimes it is soft and subtle, and sometimes it can be rough. Most of all, we see that it changes over time. We are aware of our breathing. We develop stillness of the mind awakening awareness in the mind and body. Breath is your greatest miracle that builds up concentration power. Your thoughts will have quieted down like a pond on which not even a ripple stirs.

Sacred Breath Meditation

Observe the up and down movement of the abdomen generated by breath, or keep the mind at the nose tip and observe feelings of contact of the breath. When any wandering thought or emotion appears, the meditator just perceives it, and then brings attention back to the abdomen movements or nose tip. When pain occurs, the meditators are encouraged to observe the physical pain.

Micro Breath Meditation

Sit up straight. Put your feet flat on the floor. Rest your hands on your lap. Close your eyes and breathe. Focus on your breathing. Breathe In again and repeat the sequence least three times. Be aware of your breathing. Beautiful breath connects you to the present moment.

Mindful Self-Compassion

Self-compassion requires the willingness to observe our negative thoughts and emotions with openness and clarity so that they are held in mindful awareness. Mindfulness is a non-judgmental receptive mind state in which one observes thoughts and feelings as they are, without trying to suppress or deny them. The first phrase of this mindful self-compassion practice is being aware, with an open and gentle attentiveness of whatever is there...... *You open up fully and bring the attention to the experience of this moment.... Notice feelings or physical sensations are present..... Acknowledge and name whatever is there....For instance, There is pain...fear....sadness...anger....shame.....vulnerability ....or there is tension in my jaw....my neck....my shoulders.....or There is self-criticism....Feel and acknowledge....whatever is there in this moment....Don't exclude anything....Open up gently to physical sensations, however unpleasant they may be....Allow thoughts to be there in a non-judging way, whatever their content...Kindly embrace emotions, however painful they may be.....*

A Compassionate Body Scan Meditation

The body scan meditation is a practice of building awareness of body sensations, feelings, and thoughts, which will help us to explore the foundations of mindfulness. This practice is commonly used in Mindfulness-Based Stress Reduction (MBSR) courses.

Begin by getting into a comfortable meditation position, seated on a chair comfortably that allows you to sit upright, your feet resting on the floor. Let your hands rest in your lap, and allow your eyes to close. See whether you can keep your spine tall while your muscles relax around it. Or else adopt an astronaut lying posture, guide attention sequentially observing feeling of different parts of the body, starting from the left toe, and finally to the top of the head.

Begin by bringing your awareness to the bottom of your feet as you notice the feeling of your feet resting against the floor. Maybe you notice tingling or other sensations, or maybe you don't notice much sensation at all. Just see what is happening in the moment.

Use the same tactics when faced with wandering thoughts and pains as the sitting breath meditation. With pain occasionally, one can use visualization techniques to see the pain leaving the body with the breath.

As you continue to watch the sensations in your feet, allow yourself to become aware of your breath moving in and out of your body. If it seems helpful, try to imagine your breath moving in and out through the bottom of your feet.

With each in-breath, allow your awareness to sharpen, with each out breath, allow tension and tightness to be released from your feet. Breathing in, focus your attention, breathing out release tension.

After a minute or so, move your awareness to your lower legs. Notice any sensations. Do you notice any pulsations or tingles in your legs? Can you notice the muscles in your legs? Begin to imagine your breath in and out through your muscles, and with each in breath sharpen your focus on the sensations, with each out-breath release tightness and tension.

If your mind wanders, see whether you are able to notice that your attention has shifted without judging yourself. You are seeing the nature of your mind. Observe how the thoughts move from one topic to the next. Bring your attention back to the sensations in your legs.

After a minute or so, move your attention to your upper legs, your thighs. Again notice whatever sensations are present, and if it is helpful imagine your breath moving in and out through the muscles of your thighs, releasing tightness and tension as you exhale, focusing your awareness as you inhale. Continue moving slowly up the body in this manner, spending a few minutes on various body parts. After your upper legs, you can notice your hands on your lap, your arms, your back and shoulders, your neck, your jaw, the muscles around your eyes, and your forehead noticing the sensations.

Before you finish, take a few moments to slowly scan your awareness through your body from head to toe. If you notice any areas of tightness or tension, let your awareness settle there for a few moments, breathing in and out through that tight place, and observing the sensations there. And again, when you notice your mind has wandered just observe that. Observe how thoughts flow.

Finally, settle your attention on your breath, watching the sensations as you take two or three slow, deep breaths before opening your eyes. Take a few moments to stretch in any way that feels comfortable before getting up or opening the eyes.

Foundations of Mindfulness in a Nutshell

Whether you are travelling, at work, or relaxing at home, take this moment of awareness.

1. BODY. Notice how it is positioned, if there's any tension anywhere.
2. FEELINGS. Are you having pleasant, unpleasant, or neutral feelings?
3. MIND STATES. Are you angry, loving, greedy, contented, calmed, distracted, awakened, or delusional?
4. MENTAL PHENOMENA. Your understanding of nature of reality or Four Noble Truths, and other mental phenomena.

Mindful Reflection

The following exercise will help you become aware of what you are experiencing at a given moment and learn to notice, distinguish and accept various thoughts and emotions that arise in your mind. Try to pause a few times each day to notice your experience, and observe the effects that doing so has on your life.

- Start by bringing attention to your breath and noticing the feeling of your breath entering and leaving your body. Do this for few minutes.
- Shift your attention to your external bodily sensations – notice the sounds and sights coming in through your senses. Notice other bodily sensations – temperature, the pressure of your body making contact with the floor or chair, etc.
- Then shift your attention to your internal bodily sensations – heart rate,

breathing, tension, hunger or fullness, aches and pains you may be feeling.
- Be aware of your mental experiences – notice what are you thinking, e.g., "This is odd." "What is it now." "I don't feel like this is going to work."
- Now, notice your emotions – interest. Irritation. Anticipation. Boredom. Anxiety. Notice how the content of your thoughts can impact how you feel.
- Now bring awareness to your motivation (what you want to do) and mental imagery (pictures or fantasy playing out in your mind).

Bring awareness to these experiences, noticing and accepting your thoughts, emotions, motivations and mental images as temporary events. As we do this process of mindful awareness, we will become better at recognizing these experiences for what they are – temporary experiences – rather than being carried away by them. We will also learn to notice how one mental experience can lead to the next.

How Compassion Affects the Mind

Take a moment to connect with compassion. Slow down your breathing a bit, and try to recall a time in which you were touched by suffering, perhaps of someone you cared about, and were motivated to help them. Feel this experience of wanting them to be free from suffering. Notice what is happening in your mind. what were you feeling? What were you paying attention to? What were you thinking about and telling yourself? What were you imagining? What sensations did you feel in your body (tension, activation, etc.)? What were you motivated to do? What actions did you take? Notice how compassion affects your mind.

Compassion and Emotions

"You will find that as you move from feeling threatened to feeling safe in a situation, your ability to experience and act with compassion increases."

Think of a time when you were behaving aggressively or when you refused to communicate with another person. What emotions did you feel at that time? Now think of a time when you were behaving kindly and compassionately. How did you feel then? You will find that as you move from feeling threatened to feeling safe in a situation, your ability to experience and act with compassion increases.

Working with Unwanted Thoughts and Emotions

Think of an unwanted mental experience, such as cruel thoughts you may have had about someone, angry or fearful thoughts you have experienced, or other feelings to which you usually respond with self-blame. Instead of beating ourselves up, we can respond differently:

- Accept and acknowledge the thoughts or emotion: "I notice I am enjoying how much he/ she struggling."
- Empathize with ourselves and redirect ourselves towards our goal: "It makes sense that I'd feel and think this way, given how my relationship with he/she has gone in the past. But I want to be a compassionate person, not someone who delights in other's misfortune."
- Feel good that we noticed this habit and now have the opportunity to work with it: "I want to change this kind of

habit and work to cultivate compassion in my life. Good thing I caught myself thinking this way."
- Bring up a compassionate motivation: "This is an opportunity to see the benefit of having compassion for people and to generate that compassion. Deep down, I do want he/she – and everyone else – to be happy and to not suffer."
- Gently shift our minds to a thought that reflects our commitment to compassion: "May he/she have peace and support as she copes with this challenge." Generate a compassionate thought or image in your mind, wishing the other person and yourself well, envisioning them - and you – having peace, happiness and all the conditions enabling you to be at your best.

Compassionate Practice

Consider a compassionate habit you would like to cultivate. This may be a way of thinking or approaching a situation, or a considerate behavior you would like to turn into a habit. It may involve bringing empathy into your interactions, for example by taking a moment during your conversations to pause and consider how the other person might be feeling. Come up with a plan to integrate this habit into your life. For example, you could plan to pause and consider the feelings of the other person during the first conversation you have when you get to work every day. The idea is to find a way to practice this way of thinking, feeling or behaving over and over, so that it gradually becomes a well-entrenched habit.

Cultivating Compassionate Qualities

At least once per day, bring to mind a compassionate quality you would like to develop in yourself.
- Warmth
- Contentment
- Acceptance and nonjudgment
- Confidence
- Courage
- Patience
- Humility
- Humor
- Generosity
- Loving Kindness
- Forgiveness
- Gratitude

Imagining you already have that quality, picture yourself enacting it in your life. Imagine how your motivation, emotions, reasoning, behaviour, and interactions are shaped by this quality. As you end this exercise, try to bring this quality with you as you embrace the world with compassion.

Patience

"Patience is flexible, open, and ready to respond to the world before us with compassion."

Patience, capacity, or tolerance is the helpful attitude toward accepting and working with the reality of existence. Basically, patience is simple, it means waiting. No matter how good our conduct or practice, expecting or grabbing at some reward or result is a hindrance. When we do our best without any particular expectation, we can actually be ready for whatever happens. Patience is flexible, open, and ready to respond to the world before us with compassion. When the world presents pain and suffering, when we are stuck in misery, trying to force, ourselves out of the situation may only embed us more deeply. Patience allows us the space to see some other option. But we must be willing to wait wisely.

In meditation we explore patience by learning to maintain upright posture and attitude right in the midst of our fears, confusions and anger. By developing patience, we gradually can see through emotional upheavals and gain insights. We can become open and aware of our inner conflicts and also the underlying calmness with mindfulness. Modern technological society puts a premium on speed and business, on keeping up to the nanosecond with the latest fashion. The modern world does not provide much intentional training in patience. Living in this difficult world, filled with situations of apparent suffering, cruelty, and injustice, we can develop our capacity to endure, to be patient with our life, to learn how to respond wisely and helpfully, without feeling overwhelmed or compelled to react unmindfully.

People and situations that hassle us are our great teachers. Receiving praise sometimes may be an encouragement to persevere, but flatterers are more often like thieves, stealing our opportunity for practice. Our enemies and critics show us our weaknesses and the areas where we can grow, and it is helpful to see them as guides and teachers.

The fundamental patience or tolerance is for the constant changing and conditioned nature of all phenomena. Realizing that all things are impermanent, and that all things are totally conditioned by everything else, we must be patient with the fact that we cannot ultimately rely on any separate, particular thing, person, approach, or teaching. When we try to hold on to any limited entity or idea, we cause suffering. Wisdom naturally inspires patience, and patience lets us stay calm and available to the arousal of this wisdom.

Loving kindness

"May all beings be safe,
May all beings be happy,
May all beings be healthy,
May all beings live with ease."

Loving kindness is a universal practice. The foundation of loving kindness is acceptance of ourselves and others. As a teacher of meditation and creative writing, I try to begin classes by radiating loving kindness. The phrases we choose are expressions of the very powerful force of intention in our minds. Every time we silently say one of the phrases, we are harnessing the power of intention. Cultivating loving kindness goes against the grain of our habitual patterns, so it is important to do the meditation regularly. There is a power beyond words- a power that can't be denied- and incorporating the loving kindness meditation regularly into our practice life allows us to tap into this power.

Loving Kindness Meditation

Take time to establish yourself in boundless love. Pay attention to the feeling of kindness, softness, warmth, and gentleness in the heart. Cultivate and bring this quality into consciousness as if boundless love were a muscle that has not been used.

Be aware of the posture, making sure the body is not tense. Soften, relax the body. Pay attention to the posture so that one isn't too tight, too strained. If there is a feeling of tightness or tension, draw the feeling of boundless love around that tension. Allow tension to disappear, by drawing boundless love around you. Surround yourself with goodwill and allow the tension to disappear into the feeling of boundless goodwill.

First begin by sending goodwill to yourself, which open our hearts to others. The best thing we can do for our own anger – to be cheerful and patient and kind. Have gratitude, generosity and appreciation. We are doing them a big favour by taking care of ourselves first. They will be very grateful to us if we take care of our anger and stress, and become peaceful and happy. When you take care of yourself, you take care of the whole world. And when you take care of the world, you take care of yourself. If you walk down the street with peace in your heart, there is peace in Canada. If you walk down the street with joy in *your heart, there is joy in Sri Lanka. Use the following phrases to grow with boundless love:*

*"May I be safe,
May I be happy,
May I be healthy,
May I live with ease."*

After directing goodwill to yourself, you move on to someone you find inspiring, or to whom you feel grateful. Bring the person's presence into your mind and direct the loving phrases toward him or her:

*"May you be safe,
May you be happy,
May you be healthy,
May you live with ease."*

In the final phase we offer goodwill to all beings everywhere. The boundless love you feel for your child or partner should be extended out into the world to include everyone, even those people you do not like, or who do not like you and to all beings. Therein lies the challenge. It is easy to altruistically love your baby, not so easy to feel that same love for a stranger on the other side of the planet, particularly when that stranger lives in a filthy, far distant place where people definitely need love. Goodwill should be unconditional, since conditional love creates its own opposite, something you dislike or even hate. Boundless love extends to all corners of the Earth, from the highest mountain to the deepest ocean, the coldest place to the hottest desert. There is nowhere that your love does not reach and permeate and nourish.

Boundless love is the product of a liberated boundless heart, it is the highest, most sublimely beautiful energy of all, and it leads to the cessation of suffering and enlightenment. It is truly boundless, and you are capable of not just experiencing it in your own life, but also to generate vast amounts of it and send it out into the world.

"May all beings be safe,
May all beings be happy,
May all beings be healthy,
May all beings live with ease"

Loving Kindness Meditations

"May I be safe,
May I be happy,
May I be healthy,
May I live with ease."

"May you be safe,
May you be happy,
May you be healthy,
May you live with ease."

"May all beings be safe,
May all beings be happy,
May all beings be healthy,
May all beings live with ease."

Micro Loving Kindness Meditation

"I wish for this person to be happy."

Blessings of Loving Kindness Meditation

The more we open our hearts to all beings, the happier our lives will be. Buddha taught that those who practice loving kindness experience eleven benefits.

1. You sleep well
2. You awaken easily
3. You enjoy pleasant dreams
4. People love you
5. Celestial beings love you
6. The devas protect you
7. You are safe from external dangers
8. Your face is radiant
9. Your mind is serene
10. You will be unconfused at the moment of death
11. You will take rebirth in the higher, happier realms

Forgiveness

"Forgiveness is giving up the possibility of a better past."

*"May I forgive myself for ... ,
May I forgive you for ... ,
May you forgive me for .... "
- Meditation on Forgiveness*

It may be easy for us to be kind, and also forgiving when life is going well. But it is only when life gets difficult that the depth of our spiritual practice is revealed. For our kindness to be real, it can't depend on how others treat us, or on how we feel at any given moment. Truthfully, when we feel mistreated, kindness is often the farthest thing from our minds and hearts. Yet, for genuine happiness to be possible, we ultimately have to go to that deep place within us where true kindness and forgiveness can be accessed.

The first step in forgiveness is to feel the remorse of going against our own heart, our own true nature. At some point we develop the understanding that by holding onto our resentment we are hurting ourselves, perhaps even more than other person is hurting us.

The practice of forgiveness allows us to reconnect with our own hearts: but the only way to actually engage in a forgiveness practice is to persevere, coming back to our experience again and again, letting layer after layer of anger and fear fall away in the process. Forgiveness cleans up the emotional wound.

The path to forgiveness is a way of opening up to the possibilities of true healing so that you can send loving kindness to yourself and to others. Forgiveness is a soft gentle way of learning how to lovingly accept whatever arises and to leave it be, without trying to control it with your thoughts.

Forgiveness Meditation

Sit down comfortably with your eyes closed or open. The first step of this practice is to forgive yourself by taking the following four statements one at a time, such as

"I forgive myself for not understanding"
"I forgive myself for making mistakes"
"I forgive myself for causing pain to myself or anyone else"
"I forgive myself for not acting the way I should have acted"

Place that feeling of forgiveness in your heart and radiate the feeling through repetition. Initially you will face resistance to forgive yourself. By recognizing, repeating, and relaxing you can return back to a peaceful state of mind and start repeating it with a smile.

The next step is to forgive other people for not understanding, making mistakes, for causing pain to themselves and to you, or for not acting in the way they should have acted. Forgive them for everything.

Visualize them in your mind and look into their eyes and forgive them. Keep repeating one of these statements or you can make up your own statement of forgiveness if it seems right.

It is best to forgive them by using the same statement over and over again.

"I forgive you for…"

Whenever mind becomes distracted, softly, gently recognize the distraction and comeback with repeating and relaxing with a smile.

After a period of time, then change things around and hear that person forgiving you for… Still look into their eyes and hear them say

"I forgive you too. I really do forgive you".

This forgiveness path starts by forgiving yourself, forgiving another person, and then, you hear them forgive you too.

Put forgiveness into everything all of the time. This will develop a loving-acceptance and a true feeling of love toward every situation and every person that caused so much pain. The pain will diminish until there is only a memory of that situation or of that person without any experience of grief. It is necessary to keep this practice going for quite some time so that eventually, upon retraining the mind you rewire the brain so that all attachments will be let go of automatically.

Micro Forgiveness Meditation

"May I forgive myself for ... ,
May I forgive you for ... ,
May you forgive me for ...."

Generosity

"A generous heart
Kind speech
And a life of service and compassion
Are the things which renew
humanity."
-The Buddha

Generosity is the very first quality of an enlightened mind. It is the wealth of enlightened beings. Along with faith, morality, moral shame, moral dread, listening skills, and wisdom it gives wealth beyond measure. The Noble Eightfold Path begins because of the joy that arises from a generous heart. Pure unhindered delight flows freely when we practice generosity. Also, it is a way to overcome greediness through a generous heart. We experience happiness in forming the intention to give, in the actual act of giving, and in recollecting the fact that we have given.

If we practice joyful giving, we will open our lives to the miracles of spiritual growth and well-being. The practice of generosity is about creating space. We see our limits, and we extend them continuously and consciously, joyfully, which creates expansiveness and spaciousness of mind. We practice generosity to free the mind from delusion, to weaken the forces of craving and clinging which takes us from one mirage to another.

We also practice generosity to free others, to extend welfare and happiness to all beings, to somehow-as much as each one of us can-lessen the suffering in this world. When our practice of generosity is genuine, when it's complete, we realize inner spaciousness and peace, and we can awakened our harmonious lives, extending boundless caring for all beings.

The Buddha said that when we offer someone food, we are not just giving that person something to eat; we are giving something more. We are giving them strength, health, beauty, and clarity of mind, even life itself, because none of those things is possible without food.

In a single moment of offering someone food, open your heart with love, compassion, and joy. In that moment of giving we are abandoning ill will, aversion and delusion as we perform a wholesome or skillful action. We come to the understanding that what we do in our life-the choices we make, by giving materially, by time, by service and by care the values we hold will create harmony in the world. In one moment of true giving our habitual thought patterns will fall away and we become one and boundless.

Gratitude

"Be grateful for everything in your life, and your face will come to shine like a star, and everyone who sees it will be made glad and peaceful. Persist in gratitude, and Love will shine through you its all-healing joy."

As we have seen with attention practices, when we pay attention, anything can be interesting. This will set your life in new direction.

You don't have to wait for appreciation and gratitude to spontaneously arise. You can consciously cultivate this powerful ally to a joyful heart. Each day of your life, you have many opportunities to develop a grateful heart by paying attention to the blessings, big and small, that are all around you. Even if things are uncomfortable, or not as you might wish, it is still possible to find something you can be grateful for.

Each year I visit my relatives in Sri Lanka during my vacation period. When the day of travel comes, I usually become stressed out. After making my long travel times, I began to fall into a spiral of self-blame. But with the cultivation of mindfulness and gratefulness, I quickly saw what was happening in my mind. I decided to enjoy the airport: the bookstore, the food, the people around, the wireless connection.

Anyone who develops a more refined sense of gratitude in life will gradually feel a deep appreciation to everything around, the forests, fields, streams, rivers and the paths and roads and everything in the world, the flowers and the unknown birds flying here and there all around us. In addition, the streams and marshes dry up because the forests, where the water reserves naturally gather, have all gone. Without the forests and the flowing streams, the clouds can no longer form and build up to release their abundant rains. Fruit trees are cut down whole, so their entire worth is reduced to what can be harvested that one time. If people simply had gratitude in their hearts, then these things couldn't happen. The things which gladden the mind would be plentiful all over the earth and everywhere we would live at ease. Being grateful for all the things our planet provides us with, we would cherish, nurture and foster its welfare. Be grateful for your life on earth which is very short and precious and has the potential to enlighten you if you pay enough attention to awaken from the dream of existence.

Gratitude Meditation

Take a few minutes to think of some of the people and things you feel gratitude for in your life. You might begin with being grateful that you can read this book. Your thoughts and feelings as you savour a cup of tea. Giving thanks to the water that nourishes you also opens the tap on your own sense of gratitude in your life, even for the very small things, like a cup of tea. Be grateful for the teachings of mindfulness. As each person, quality, or thing comes up in your imagination, say silently to yourself, "I am grateful to …. Or for…." Pause with each thought to feel the experience of gratitude that arises in your body and mind. Let gratitude flow.

Before you finish with this exercise, stop and take in the fullness of the feeling of gratitude itself. Breathe it in deeply, and let it pervade your body and mind.

Practice of Gratitude

- Make thoughtful thank you notes a part of how you communicate with others.
- Send specific and timely notes of appreciation.
- Acknowledge the value of contributing.
- Use the right kind of touch.

"Let us be grateful to the people who make us happy; they are the charming gardeners who make our lives blossom."

"Be grateful for everything in your life and your face will come to shine like a star. Everyone who sees it will be made glad and peaceful. Persist in gratitude, and Love will shine through you with its all-healing joy."

"Cultivating gratitude, may we be fully present for the many blessings in our lives even the smallest wonders."

"You become more grateful by repeatedly installing experiences of gratitude."

How You Show Your Gratitude

If you consider that long list of people and things that you are grateful for, take a few minutes to write mindfully now about how you might show your gratitude in your own way. Perhaps you might wish to say thank you to the environment around you by consciously using less plastic, or you might thank a loved one by calling them at the weekend.

Harmlessness

"The world does not know that we must all come to an end here; but those who know it, their quarrels cease at once."

Harmlessness is a peaceful practice born out of understanding, love, and compassion. As a person born in Sri Lanka I was always drawn into practice of harmlessness from my early childhood. I took care even not to harm an ant or mosquito as a practice of this beautiful way of living which later led me to become a vegetarian. It was the underlying principle of Gandhi's revolution and of his personal meditation practice. It is a good way to relate to the world and to oneself to create peace. Why not try to live without harming any living being. If we lived that way each moment, we wouldn't have the insane levels of violence in the world today. And we would be more generous toward ourselves as well. You can start practicing harmlessness on yourself and with others in each moment of your compassionate life.

The willingness to harm or hurt comes ultimately out of fear. Non-harming requires that you see your own fears and that you understand them and own them mindfully with cultivating loving kindness, and compassion. Harmlessness is the way to World Peace.

*"If you can't have compassion to your enemy,
Start with your wife, or husband, or your children,
Try to put their welfare first and your own last each moment and let the circle of compassion expand from there."*

Contentment

"If we are looking for outer conditions to bring us contentment, we are looking in vain."

Happiness and enlightenment are feelings filled with peace and contentment. You can create heaven on earth if you accept yourself just the way you are right now, when you renounce everything, let go everything and completely surrender. When I left behind all my material belongings and migrated to Canada, I totally renounced everything and surrendered to a new world. This experience of renunciation helped me overcome a mind that wanted to hold on, creating happiness and enlightenment within.

"We rejoice when we see others at happiness, but we rejoice in our own well-being as well. The seed of true happiness grows out of contentment, gratitude, hope and love. In lasting happiness, you feel part of the flow of life, you feel a sense of connection. For most people, happiness represents feelings of pleasure, delight, gladness and aliveness."

Lasting joy, happiness, and enlightenment comes from strong sense of contentment, regardless of whether or not we achieve what we are striving for. Most people seek contentment by striving to obtain everything they want, including the perfect body, mate, money, house, and cars. But this does not work. Contentment is to want and appreciate what we have.

On our daily journey there is an inexhaustible number of moments-opportunities to experience happiness and joy. On my early morning journey to work I walk paying attention, I breathe deeply as I look up at colorful clouds aglow from the morning sun. The more aware I am, the more likely I am to experience joyful moments along the way. Looking back on each day, I am reminded how easy it is to be in such a hurry that we miss moments of joy. These moments, whether they are long or brief, happens only when we stop and remain calm.

"Contentedness the best riches."

The cultivation of contentment is a stepping stone to our compassionate life. There is always something else to want, even before we take a moment to appreciate what we already have, or are about to have. We need to loosen our grasping and our clinging, and we need to have the courage to step out of our conditioning and awaken from our dream of existence. When we overcome our habitual seeking and restlessness we could be satisfied with what we have where we are. Contentment will open you up to see the abundance we could experience right now, right here. You could awaken joy with a glimpse of a cherry blossom, eyes of a child and their beauty will open your heart. As soon as you begin to fully enjoy all little joys in life you become more and more grateful to the world around you. If we practice this gratefulness each moment of our life the overall happiness in life will be greatly increased. My regular noting of things that I am grateful for transformed my experiences and resulted in a joyful and happy life.

We could easily loose our contentment with our habitual seeking and restlessness, our easy dissatisfaction with where we are if we are not mindful.

One day I was walking to work and passed berry trees in full and magnificent bloom. My heart just swelled at their beauty. Whenever I remembered the short glimpse of berry trees joy arised in my mind.

> *"He who lives without looking for pleasures, his senses well controlled, moderate in his food, faithful and strong."*

We can't hold on to earthly pleasures any more than we can hold on to anything or anyone. Trying to hold on in a constantly changing world is futile, and it pulls us out of the moment. Yet we do it all the time. To begin with, we hold on to our material goods. There may be a lucky few of us who live simply and without a lot of things, but if you are at home look around you. You've probably got a ton of reasons for hanging on to most of the objects you see.

That's just the external world. Our inner world is even more filled with stuff we hold on to- our ideas of what we think life is about, who we think is right, or how things are supposed to be. When any of these important things are threatened, our world can feel like it might crumble. Relationships change, favourite things break, and pets die. All conditioned things are impermanent in nature. Trying to hold on to the way we want life to be only leads to frustrations and disappointments. Circumstances change, we change, things change, and letting go of what we're holding on to can be a great relief. Do not fear of arising of good or bad thoughts, as thinking makes it so.

"Vegetarianism"
Mindful Compassionate Eating

"By calling wise attention to your body's signals with eating, you will curb cravings, and feed your body what it truly needs."

Vegetarianism is the practice of abstaining from the consumption of meat (red meat, poultry, seafood, and the flesh of any other animal), and may also include abstention from by-products of animal slaughter, born out of compassion.

Our practice of eating begins with an awareness of our wise effort. We need food for survival and for well-being, yet our consumption is often based on some unmet need of greediness. Overeating may easily cause feelings of regret, as well as irrational perceptions or mental formations. Learning to guard the garden of our consciousness is the best preventive medicine for both physical and emotional well-being. Unmindful consumption leads to suffering. One way to transform at root level is to be mindful of the overall impact of what, why, and how we consume. This awareness helps us realize that the psychological nutrients we consume affect our ability to compassionate and be happy. Awareness creates the correct nourishment, healing support, and ethical ground for a joyful life born out of compassion.

Mindful Eating Meditation

Try eating a meal with attention, in silence. Slow down your movements enough so that you can watch the entire process carefully.

Observe the colours and texture of your food. Contemplate where this food comes from and how it was grown or made. Is it harmful? Does it come from animal slaughter? Is it synthetic? Does it come from a factory? Was anything put into it? Can you see the efforts of all the other people who were involved in bringing it to you? Can you see how it was once connected with nature? Can you see the natural elements and the sunlight and the rain in your vegetables, fruits, and grains?

Ask yourself if you want this food in your body before you eat it. How much of it do you want in your belly? Listen to your body while you are eating. Can you detect when it says enough? What do you do at this point? What impulses come up in your mind?

Be aware of how your body feels in the hours after you have eaten. Does it feel heavy or light? Do you feel tired or energetic? Do you have unusual amounts of gas or other symptoms of dysregulation? Can you relate these symptoms to particular foods or combinations of foods to which you might be sensitive?

When shopping, try reading labels on food items such as cereal boxes, breads, and frozen foods. What is in them? Are they high in fat, or in animal fat? Do they have salt and sugar added? What are the first ingredients listed?

Be aware of your cravings, ask yourself where they come from. What do you really want? What are you going to get from eating that particular food? Can you eat just a little of it? Are you addicted to it? Can you try letting go of it this once, and just watch the craving as a thought or feeling? Can you think of something else to do in the moment that will be healthier and more personally satisfying than eating?

When preparing food, are you doing it mindfully? Can you be totally present with food preparation? Try being aware of your breathing and your whole body as you do so. What are the effects of doing things this way?
Look around for alternatives if you decide that they are no longer what you want to be cooking.

"Be aware of the stress and suffering caused by unwise consumption. Be committed to cultivating good health, both physical and mental, for yourself, your family, and your society by practicing wise eating, drinking, and consuming. Practice looking deeply into your consumption of the four kinds of nutriments- edible foods, sense impressions, volition, and consciousness."

Mindful Eating – In a nutshell

- Preparation (of the food with wise attention)
- Arriving (in the present moment, e.g., breath)
- Looking deeply (gratitude)
- Intention (to eat wisely)
- Choosing
- Seeing (textures, color, shape)
- Smelling
- Placing (in the mouth)
- Savoring (chewing, tasting, swallowing)
- Fullness (how the food feels in the belly)

Post- Eating Reflection

1. How was this experience compared to how you normally eat? What insights, if any, arose?
2. What stood out most to you?
3. How can you incorporate vegetarianism into your everyday life?

Open Your Heart like a Flower

"While walking you consider the act of each step you take as an infinite wonder, and a joy will open your heart like a flower, enabling us to enter the world of reality."

In the vast cosmological scheme, it is rare and precious to be born as a human being. To walk on earth is the greatest miracle in your life. Take this precious short time on earth to fully experience its beauty. Walk slowly and leisurely in a garden, along a river, along a farm, or on a village path. Be aware of the beauty around, sensing freshness of the air you breathe in. You see the wonder of light and shade as the sun shines through the leaves swaying in the breeze. You feel the touch of your feet on the ground and the miracle of your walk on earth.

Walking Meditation

Focus your attention to your soles of the feet, on the sensations and feelings as they arise and pass away. As you walk, the feeling will change. As the foot is lifted and comes down again into contact with earth, a new feeling arises. Be aware of this sensation on the sole of the foot. Again as the foot lifts, mentally note the new feeling as it arises. When you lift each foot and place it down, know the sensations felt. At each step, certain new feelings are experienced and old feelings cease. With each step on earth there is a new experienced-feeling arising and feeling passing away. We are aware of whatever type of feelings arise at the soles of the feet. This is a type of meditation called, walking meditation, in which one can focus and concentrate the mind or develop investigative knowledge and wisdom to awakening. As so much of life is taken up with the activity of walking, if you know how to apply awareness to it then even simply walking to work or walking about in your house can become a wonderful act of calming and enlightening. According to Buddha's teachings, this precious act of walking develops the following benefits:

1. Endurance for walking long distances
2. It is good for striving
3. It is healthy
4. It is good for digestion
5. The concentration won from walking meditation lasts a long time.

This wonderful act of walking will help you to overcome drowsiness by developing a heightened sense of alertness, effort, and zeal. We are bringing the mind to the here and now. See how you can develop the happiness born from serenity and awareness as you are walking. Once your attention is fully focused on the experience of walking, you will find this is a very pleasant experience. As your attention increases, you will know more of the sensations of walking. Then you find that walking does have this sense of beauty and peace to it. Every step becomes a beautiful step. This will awaken peacefulness, a sense of stillness, a sense of the mind being very comfortable and very happy in its own miraculous nature. The miracle is not to walk on water. The miracle is to walk on the green earth in the present moment.

"At each step, certain new feelings are experienced and old feelings cease. With each step on earth there is a new feeling experienced-feeling arising, feeling passing away; feeling arising, feeling passing away. We are aware of whatever type of feelings arises at the soles of the feet."

10 Step Walk

You can use a short 10 step walk to de-stress at work. When your mind wanders during the 10 steps, bring it back to the awareness of walking. Each step can be broken down by mentally repeating lifting, shifting, placing. Lift the heel, shift the foot forward, and then place it down. The focus is on the soles of the feet and repeating the process will help center you and help you let go of all the stress-inducing aspects of life.

Post-Walking Reflection

1. How was this experience compared to how you normally walk? What insights, if any, arose?
2. What stood out most to you?
3. How can you incorporate walking, or movement in general, into your everyday life?

Rewiring Your Brain for Compassion

"You become more compassionate by repeatedly installing experiences of compassion."

When the sun began to set in the true north of this precious planet, I was walking along the beach. I stopped and sat staring at the setting sun, wind gently ruffling my hair. I picked up my notepad and began to write this chapter.

"Beautiful sunset, shiny pebbles on the beach, touch of my feet on sand, rustling leaves, sounds of birds, sunshine on eyelashes, clean air."

The list reminded me of all the natural and positive things I experienced. I realized if we could focus on the present moment and on natural pleasures, life was good. After pausing to watch the sunset for a few moments more, I walked with awareness towards my home. I was enjoying my precious life with peace, contentment, boundless love, compassion and awareness. Although I was experiencing the suffering of life, it had diminished greatly – mainly because, I had eliminated so much secondary suffering with my mindful practices This reminded me the wisdom of Buddha's teachings on wise effort, and what my Positive Neuroplasticity guru and renowned

Neuropsychologist, Dr. Rick Hanson teaches. I was discovering that it was possible to find pleasure amid my suffering. I managed to find happiness and meaning while enduring hardships of living. I was embracing life mindfully. I was taking in the good.

Neuroscience is now showing the underlying tendencies in the brain that can make it hard to enjoy life – and maintain optimism while in pain and illness. It has also become clear that you can began to appreciate life once again with mindfulness and compassionate practices.

It is a sad reality that we humans are hardwired to suffer. Buddha's First Noble Truth is that there is suffering in life. Suffering arises due to greed, hatred, and delusion. According to Dr. Rick Hanson, we have a negativity bias. Even though our species (for the most part) no longer has to outrun wild animals, our brains are still hardwired to cling to the bad in life instead of the good. As many of us know, negative thinking comes with negative health effects impacted by our stress, worry, and anxiety.

Dr. Rick Hanson says that we can use the science of positive neuroplasticity (PNP) to train our brains to take in the good. He illustrates how through changing our frame of mind we can, in turn, reframe our brain. From there, our re-trained brain is primed to take on a more positive state of mind, and reap physical and mental well-being.

It is well understood from the famous quote by neuropsychologist Donald Hebb, *"neurons that fire together wire together"*. What this means is that the areas of our brains that we use the most often become stronger. Knowing this, Dr. Hanson writes that we can take advantage of fleeting, everyday positive moments to combat our innate negativity biases.

In his teachings on Positive Neuroplasticity (PNP) and his book *Hardwiring Happiness*, Dr.

Hanson outlines a four-step method to get in the habit of taking in the good:

> **Have a positive experience.** Notice something positive that's happening to you, or create a positive experience for yourself by reminiscing on something that brings you gratitude or joy (for example, recognize a task you've completed and are proud of. Or recognize a compassionate action).
>
> **Enrich it.** Stay with this positive feeling for at least five seconds. Encourage the positive feeling to become intense, recognize how it's relevant and how it nourishes you.
>
> **Absorb it.** Let this experience sink into your mind—or as Dr. Rick Hanson writes—"place it like a jewel in the treasure chest of your heart."

Link the positive experience with something negative. (This step is optional.) Use your current, vivid feeling of positivity to heal old pain. For example, if you're currently feeling included and liked, you can touch on a past time when you felt lonely.

Much of our suffering is a side effect of the instincts that nature has built into us through millions of years of evolution. Our attention inevitably focuses on threats. Our inherent bias towards negative thinking ensures that we tend to see threats everywhere and notice the flaws in everything out of ignorance. This is the main reason that the mind focuses on pain and suffering with laser sharpness. We do not simply notice the overwhelming number of simple and pleasant things in our lives.

In his teachings, Dr. Rick Hanson describes the brain as possessing, "velcro for negative experiences and Teflon for good ones." For example, the amygdala, central to the brain's alarm system, dedicates two-thirds of its neurons to processing negative experiences. According to the studies done by John Cacioppo, Ph.D., at the University of Chicago, this was evident. He showed people pictures known to arouse positive feelings (say, a Ferrari, or a pizza), those certain to stir up negative (a mutilated face or dead cat), and those known to produce neutral feelings (a plate, a hair dryer). Meanwhile he recorded electrical activity in the brain's cerebral cortex that reflected the magnitude of information processing that took place. The brain, Cacioppo demonstrated, reacts more strongly to stimuli it deems negative. There is a greater surge in electrical activity. Thus, our attitudes are more heavily influenced by downbeat news than good news. These findings demonstrated negative experiences generate intense activity, while pleasant ones of equal magnitude produce far less. This bias is reflected in the body's hormonal systems too. We have numerous stress hormones that force us to respond to negative experience, cortisol, adrenaline, and norepinephrine are all fast acting and have powerful effects on the body. The equivalent positive ones, such as the cuddle hormone oxytocin, lack the same potency and urgency, although it does have powerful effects in the long run, enhancing, health, healing, and well-being.

Understandingly the negative bias is the first step toward rebalancing. The next step is to gently soothe the brain networks that maintain the bias and that ultimately lead to unnecessary pain and suffering. As these networks begin to calm down, you can then begin strengthening the brain circuits that notice and appreciate life. This rebalancing will help you to see more clearly, act more effectively, and be less distracted and rattled by day-to-day life with wise understanding. It will also create a sense of open hearted calmness. As this sense of tranquility builds, it will further reduce your pain and suffering, while dissolving feelings of anxiety, stress, unhappiness, and exhaustion through awakening.

Rebalancing is achieved by bringing mindful and open-hearted awareness to life and focusing awareness on mindful practices. This may all seem a little fluffy, but it is grounded in solid neuroscience. The Canadian psychologist Donald Hebb said, *"Neurons that fire together wire together."* So with mindful awareness, you are encouraging the parts of your brain that notice and create the sensations of happiness and joy to grow and become stronger – to *"wire together."* This is evident by one of the great discoveries of recent years – that the brain is highly plastic, which means that it is constantly adapting and changing its architecture. In an article in Psychology Today, Rebecca Gladding, a clinical instructor and attending, psychiatrist at UCLA, an expert in anxiety, depression, and mindfulness, explained the mechanisms by which engaging in 15 to 30 minutes of daily meditation restructured the connections between various regions of the brain, thereby affecting how we react to and process the world around us. We can change our brain for the better with mindfulness. If the brain is constantly adapting and changing, we might as well encourage it to move in the right direction.

The term neuroplasticity refers to the brain's capacity to change in response to experience. Thanks to latest neuroscience discoveries, we now understand that the brain is constantly rewiring itself, throughout our life. This feature of brain Neuroplasticity simply means that the brain (neuro-) can change or adapt (-plasticity).

Practices such as compassion and mindfulness does change the brain. Everything we do changes the brain. We meditate with heart and mind. With any physical exercise and repetition of certain body movements, the body becomes stronger, more efficient and better able to perform those movements with ease. A similar process can occur with the brain: with the engagement and repetition of certain mental processes, the brain becomes more efficient at those processes. In other words, experience and cultivating can lead to functional and structural reorganization of the brain. This cultivation is called meditation.

From a therapeutic point of view, it means that we can unwire unwholesome thoughts and behavior and wire in wholesome ones through wise effort and wise mindfulness.

We can change our brains with mental practice, and when the brain changes certain experiences becomes more likely than others. So we can use our minds to change our brains, which will change our minds. Dr. Richard Davidson and his team have been studying the influence of the practice of meditation and compassion on the brain. A study amongst long term meditators (Tibetan monks) showed that there are significant differences between long-term compassion meditation practitioners, compared with beginners, in the brain function on the electroencephalogram, particularly in gamma activity and neural synchronicity (Lutz, Greischar, Rawlings, Ricard, and Davidson, 2004). Independent of the circumstances, those who had undergone a more intensive training could evoke loving and compassionate feelings more easily. A subsequent study with fMRI, which gives more detailed information on the activity of different brain regions, revealed that the practice of compassion towards others produced changes in the brain areas that are associated with empathy and emotion regulation.

Research with fMRI has become increasingly sophisticated and recent data shows that the practice of mindful or focused attention affects other brain regions than the practice of compassion or loving kindness (goodwill), which particularly affects areas relating to experience of positive emotions and emotional processing when faced with distress. Results suggests that effect of meditation grow with the level of practice and are also transferred to non-meditative states.

"Be with what is there,

Decrease the negative,

Increase the positive."

"Witness,

Pull weeds,

Plant flowers."

"Let be,

Let go,

Let in."

"Wise attention is present in all three,

We also need "wise effort."

Interconnectedness

The Buddha is known for the miraculous power of understanding thoroughly the mind of others. This is possible because the basic working principles of the mind are the same in everyone.

Neuroscience has found that there are mirror neurons in animal brains that enable them to feel what others are feeling. Whether neuroscientists are able to locate this mirror neuron system in human or not, we know with certainty that we feel what others are feeling, and their feelings affect us greatly. Sometimes you walk into a room and the mere presence of a particular person may suddenly make you feel threatened or defensive.

We are interconnected, feeling what others feel in our own body and mind. However it is only with mindfulness that we are able to respond compassionately and appropriately. With mindful breathing, you can relax your body and mind so that you aren't compelled to react to that feeling or to that person through your thoughts, words, and bodily actions. Mindfulness is also protective, helping us to remain compassionate to others when they are depressed without internalizing their depression within ourselves.

Heart Mind Connection

"Wandering nerve is the superhighway for sensory information."

The story goes that Tibetan monks who were the subjects in studies on the effects of meditation and compassion practice had a lot of fun when they were hooked up to the machines. They thought it was hilarious that scientists who wanted to explore the mind placed the electrodes on their heads and not on their hearts. Is this a western tendency to focus on the brain, even when we study experiences of the heart? Meanwhile, there is strong scientific support that there are intimate neuroendocrine connections between the brain and the heart. The vagus (or wandering) nerve and its branches represent a major part of the parasympathetic autonomic nervous system and connect the brain with the inner organs and particularly the heart.

Parasympathetic, serves as the brake of the Automatic Nervous System (ANS) while the sympathetic, acts as the body's accelerator. The sympathetic nervous system (SNS) is responsible for arousal, including the fight-or-flight response. Almost two thousand years ago the Roman physician Galen gave it the name sympathetic because he observed that it functioned with the emotion (sympathos). The SMS moves blood to the muscles for quick action, partly by triggering the adrenal glands to squirt out adrenalin, which speed up the heart and increase blood pressure.

The second branch of the ANS is the parasympathetic (against emotions) nervous system (PNS), which promotes self-preservative functions like digestion and wound healing. It triggers the release of acetylcholine to put a brake on arousal, slowing the heart down, relaxing muscles, and returning breathing to normal.

When you take a deep breath, you activate the SNS. The resulting burst of adrenaline speeds up your heart, which explains why many athletes take a few short, deep breaths before starting competition. Exhaling, in turn activates the PNS, which slows down the heart. If you take a yoga or a meditation class, your instructor will probably urge you to pay particular attention to the exhalation, since deep, long breaths out help calm you down.

Loving Kindness to Calm Your Mind

Bring your attention to the breath and follow every in-and-out breath with a relaxed attention, with a kind and caring attitude. Allow a soothing breathing rhythm. You can,
- Gently and intentionally slow down and deepen the breath if it is quick, without forcing.
- Adjust your posture so that it supports a calm breathing rhythm: allow your muscles to soften, allow a soft smile.
- Follow the breath in your belly and let the belly become soft.
- Intentionally breathe through the heart area and allow feelings of space, lightness, and warmth – you can place one or both hands on your heart to help with this;
- Allow an image to form that supports a calm breathing rhythm. For example, a safe place, a soothing colour, relaxing music, or somebody whose presence calms you.

You can now become aware of the body as a whole, the breathing body that is sitting, standing or lying down. See if you can hold a kind gentle or supporting wish for yourself. For example,

"May I be .....safe......healthy.....happy...at ease....
Let these phrases come from your heart. You can let them flow through the body on the rhythm of the breath. With each inhalation you could hold the first half of the wish, and with each exhalation you could hold the second half of the wish. For example, "May I...." (on the in-breath) "....be safe" (on the out-breath).

Let a kind wish for yourself flow through you in a soft, natural way, on the rhythm of the breath or independently of the breath if that feels better.

Now after sometime you can extend the exhalation for longer time than the inhalation to activate the parasympathetic nervous system of your brain. For example, "May I...." (on the shorter in-breath) "....be safe" (on the longer out-breath).

Then you could perhaps take this caring and calm attention and good intentions with you, or remind yourself of them later in the day.

Extend the Exhalation

The parasympathetic nervous system (PNS) manages exhaling and slows your heart rate, while the sympathetic nervous system handles inhaling and speeds up the heart. If you lengthen your exhalation, that naturally engages the PNS. For several breaths or more, try counting softly in your mind to make your exhalation longer than your inhalation. For example, inhale for 1-2-3 and then exhale for 1-2-3-4-5-6.

As we breathe, we continually speed up and slow down the heart, and because of that the interval between two successive heartbeats is never precisely the same. A measurement called heart rate variability (HRV) can be used to test the flexibility of this system, and good HRV – the more fluctuation, the better – is a sign that the brake and accelerator in your arousal system are both functioning properly and in balance. Measurement of HRV is used to treat PSTD.

The pounding heart of a marathon runner is enormously different from the near cessation of the heart during the deep meditation of a meditator. On a subtler level, your heart responds to the stimulation of daily stresses, even the most minor. If you grow tense, your heart beat becomes more like a steady drumming, quick and evenly spaced. In medical terms, this means your HRV a low, which isn't preferable. High HRV occurs when the heart responds within a flexible range of faster or slower beats depending on what's happening in the bodymind. (The Healing Self- Deepak Chopra, and Rudolph E. Tanzi).

Rhythms of the Heart

"A healthy heart is flexible and changes its rhythm according to the situation."

The newer branches of the vagus developed in a way that could support soothing and attachment behavior. An increase in parasympathetic activity or vagal tone can be measured as an increase in the physiological arrhythmia of the heart rate as it correlates with the breathing rhythm. In a calm state with optimal balance between sympathetic and parasympathetic activity, every in-breath is accompanied by an acceleration of the heart rate and every out breath by a deceleration. An increase in heart rate variability (HRV) correlates with the natural state of feeling contented and connected. When one feels stressed, the sympathetic tone overrules, which is accompanied by a decrease in HRV.

Compassion is a capacity that is grounded in the ability to soothe and care for others and for oneself and is dependent on these physiological systems. A powerful vagal tone means autonomic flexibility and correlates with the capacity of the parasympathetic nervous system to calm the body after it has become aroused in stressful circumstances because of threat or excitement. It does this by regulating respiration, heart rate and blood pressure and enhancing digestion and immune function. This state of rest and digest neutralizes the fight or flight reactions.

The vagus nerve is anatomically linked not only to visceral organs, but also to nerves involved in coordinating eye gaze, generating facial expressions, and tuning the ear to the frequency of the human voice. All functions that are important for forming social connections (Porges, 2007).

The vagus nerve is responsible for between 80 percent and 90 percent of impulses. In everyday language, this means that the sensory information – especially the effects of pain and stress – travelling along the body's information superhighway travels along this one nerve. As a result, when vagal nerve activity is low, a host of things could be going wrong – diminished activity is associated with increased death from infections, rheumatoid arthritis, irritable bowel syndrome, trauma, depression, and stress. Stimulating the vegus nerve has an instantaneous effect in your heart beat and HRV. (The Healing Self, Deepak Chopra and Rudolph E. Tanzi).

Although the vagal tone is a durable trait, research suggests that it can be trained in relatively short time by mental practice that enhances positive emotions such as through loving kindness meditations.

When we are in need or feeling stressed we are more likely to seek the presence and reassurance of caring others and respond with increased vagal tone and oxytocin release. Our brains and bodies are already prepared for compassion by old mechanisms that evolved when mammals adapted their survival strategies. When the neurobiological systems of this low road are well trained, a compassionate response is more likely. That is why we often start compassion exercises with a soothing breathing rhythm (increase in vagal tone and HRV), or we touch our heart with one or both hands (release of oxytocin).

When the people we love are absent we can still be caring towards ourselves and make use of soothing compassionate images. When we use our much younger capacity to bring up kind wishes and compassionate imagery, we can strengthen the neurobiological circuits. Researchers found that a few minutes of compassion-focused imagery could increase HRV and decrease the stress hormone, cortisol.

Hormone Connection

Another player in the boundless love is oxytocin. Like the vagus nerve, it plays a key role in social bonding and attachment. Although oxytocin is often called the love hormone, it is actually a neuropeptide that is produced in the brain and released in the bloodstream to have effects in the body. (Olff, 2012). Oxytocin was originally discovered to play a role during giving birth and breastfeeding. Later it became clear that the release of oxytocin facilitates social bonding in both men and women. It is released during intense and subtle kinds of pleasurable social contact, such as making love, cuddling, massaging, having a kind conversation, playing with a child, or petting a dog. It increases vagal tone and HRV (Kemp, 2012) and attenuates biological stress reactions. It is the motor behind the so called tend and befriend reaction as opposed to fight or flight (Taylor, 2006). It shifts attention from self-protection to protection of others. The boundless compassion.

The Compassionate Planet

C-O-M-P-A-S-S-I-O-N

The Compassionate Therapist

*"I thought I knew you,
But it was only me.
Then you that you truly are
Is not the you I see.
My mind has formed your image
But you have already travelled on,
I want to see only you,
But I see you through me."*

The act of helping often leads to burnout in the helpers, suggesting they forget to help themselves whilst helping others. Therapeutic work is often experienced as emotionally demanding. Compassion fatigue, more correctly called empathy fatigue and/or burnout are related and widespread phenomena in the helping professions. This can result in a drop in both job fulfilment and quality of care. The problem may start during training. It is striking that students do not gain, but lose empathic skills during their training, although empathy is generally considered to be a key therapeutic factor. The heart first pumps blood to itself before it pumps blood to other parts of the body. If this were not the case, the heart would die and subsequently the rest of the body. In the same way professional caregivers can only care well for others, after they have learned to care well for themselves. If they are unable to do so, they will suffer as well as their patients. The materialistic modern world leaves little room for compassionate practice.

But on the positive side, several mindfulness-based programs that teach health care professionals self-awareness and self-care skills have been evaluated with promising results. Particularly Mindfulness-Based Stress Reduction has a beneficial impact on their physical and mental health, quality of life, stress tolerance levels, and capacity for self-compassion. The compassionate counsellor can not only help themselves, but also their clients by meditating regularly.

Mindfulness helps therapists to both be in touch with themselves and with clients and cultivate very important skills for the therapeutic process, awareness, unconditioned regard and the capacity for compassion and holding with patience. These are therapeutic factors that offer significant contribution to a good working relationship and to therapeutic success.

It is quite likely – though research has to confirm this - that compassionate based practices in this guide will have a further positive impact. The score on the self-compassion scale seems to be even more strongly associated with mental well-being, quality of life, wisdom, personal initiative, happiness, optimism, positive emotions and dealing with stress more wisely than the score on the mindfulness scale.

We often hear from therapists who formally practice compassion and loving kindness that it helps them to experience connectedness with their clients and themselves. They feel they are better able to face the clients pain as well as their own with openness and kindness and are less bothered by feelings of countertransference. The practice supports the sense of common humanity and helps to distinguish between inevitable suffering and suffering that arise from our reactions to it.

This guide offers many insights, reflections, meditations, and practices that convey authentic ways of being present with mindfulness and compassion for the compassionate counsellor and therapist. Good health care needs both cure and care and I hope the compassion practices in this guide deepen this understanding.

"Compassion for others and self-compassion are interdependent."

Dharma Recovery

A PATH TO RECOVERYING FROM ADDICTION

"You are not alone in your difficulties and pain. You are simply experiencing human life. "

The Buddha says that the appropriate response to the First Noble Truth is to understand suffering. For the addict, this means seeing your addiction, understanding your addictive suffering, and thus beginning the recovery process. Until we see suffering and the cause of suffering, there is no possibility of change.

When we constantly avoid pain or difficulties, we are in conflict with reality. Hiding from pain, denying our failings, and ignoring suffering all requires a lot of energy and must ultimately fail. Seeing suffering evokes compassion, opening to the noble truths brings wisdom. The Buddha's noble path is not about imagining a perfect world or even trying to create utopia, but rather seeing the truths clearly and responding wisely following the Noble Eightfold Path for recovery.

We have to see suffering clearly first before we can treat it. Understanding the Four Noble Truths will help you deal with the suffering.

Write a list or narrative of the real life difficulties you face. These can range from health issues, to relationship and family problems, work problems, and financial problems. You are looking at difficulties that just come with being a human. These difficulties are what Buddha called *Dukkha* in his first Noble Truth. While you may have some influence over them, you are essentially not in control, or at least, right now, you don't see how you can control them.

Seeing this list should break any denial you have about the Truth of Suffering. It is important, though, to see your problems in the larger context of the *Dharma*, that is, to see the universal truth of suffering. You are not alone in your difficulties and pain. You are simply experiencing human life.

Now probe the ways in which you create your problems through clinging or rejecting. These may be related to your challenges. If you have financial problems, instead of trying to deal with them in practical ways, you spiral into despair. You are making the problem worse. Here we are trying to understand the cause of your difficulty. It is important to highlight the specific ways in which your addiction causes you suffering. Consider all the ways your addiction has caused you and others pain: emotional, physical, financial, and spiritual. If you are going to get into and stay in recovery, you must face the full effects of your addiction. Try to review your addiction without creating more suffering for yourself.

Now go down the list from the "Truth of Suffering", and ask yourself how you relate to each issue. If there is aversion or desire, any grasping, rejecting, or clinging, associated with an issue, and see how this clinging or aversion is causing you suffering. This is actually how we end suffering, not by ridding ourselves of problems, but by accepting the problems without being in conflict with the reality. Try, even if just for a moment, to let go of your aversion or desire and see how that feels.

For example, sending thoughts of lovingkindness to our enemy with wise intentions. This exercise eases your own heart, to let go of the painful feeling of anger and resentment. Another example is you might try to replace anxiety with calm by doing a wise concentration practice.

When you bring wise mindfulness to the clinging itself, sometimes you will let go naturally. If not, you will at least be seeing clearly how you are creating your own pain. Eventually you may give up.

When we see clearly how everything is in constant flux, we are more likely to let go, by understanding impermanence. This approach of careful investigation is one of the key elements of insight meditation. Here in this investigation process, we observe closely the details of experience and begin to detect patterns and processes within experience.

Peace and stillness have a natural cooling effect that eases our clinging. Our hearts soften, our emotions grow calm, and that to which we cling can fade away. Wise concentration practices offered in this book helps to calm the mind, along with the others steps of the Noble Eightfold Path.

The Fourth Noble Truth is the path the Buddha taught for moving towards freedom, and a model for enlightenment. This path outlined in the Noble Eightfold Path is a very systematic path. Each of the elements of the Eightfold Path is powerful and can thus be part of recovery process. The Buddha said that the wise response to the Fourth Noble Truth was to cultivate it. That means, we need to act on these principles, for our recovery as we have seen already. This means that we start to try to live our lives by the principles of the Eightfold Path. Noble Eightfold Path gives a framework for the recovery process. The Noble Eightfold Path is less a linear process than a matrix interlocking, interwoven elements. These wise practices are meant to take you to the ultimate level of human consciousness, Nirvana.

For Right View and Right Intention, we will be working mainly with contemplations and reflections. For Right Livelihood, Speech, and Action, we are more involved with daily life and our interactions with others, and with Right Effort, Mindfulness, and Concentration, the focus is meditative. This approach accomplishes several things: it brings these teachings into every facet in our lives, it gives a variety of approaches to our recovery work so that with different needs and at different stages of this work will be able to relate to and use at least some of these practices, and finally, it cultivates many different aspects of our spiritual practice, giving us a well-rounded and integrated recovery practice that leads us to wisdom and spiritual maturity.

The Process of Dharma Recovery

Although the process and sequence of recovery will vary from person to person, the following is an overview of how Dharma Recovery approach may be applied.

We begin by accepting all the ways that addiction has caused suffering in our lives and the lives of others. Turning inward and acknowledging our suffering is the beginning of the process, but it is also an ongoing practice. On a daily basis, we practice mindfulness of suffering, its causes and its cessation.

Next we investigate the underlying conditions that have influenced, and perpetuated our addictions. The causes of suffering.

Through reading, listening, studying, practicing, and reflecting the principles of the Four Noble Truths, we come to understand the possibility and potential of our own recovery. Having some hope and willingness, we take in the potential of our own recovery path.

We embark on the practice of the Noble Eightfold Path. We encourage you to begin with the practice of meditation right away. Meditation is going to be the most important tool in supporting our renunciation. Begin with the practice of focusing on your breath. After a week, you will alternate forgiveness practice with breath practice every other day. Eventually we will want you to learn and practice all the meditations offered, but we encourage you to first develop the meditation that increase concentration, that helps renunciation efforts.

As your skill in concentration increases, we begin practicing the four foundations of mindfulness and the heart practices of loving kindness, compassion, sympathetic joy, and equanimity, the four immeasurables.

Next we refine right understanding, intentions, and livelihood. This is a gradual path. No one changes overnight, but we all must continue to practice, study, act, and reflect wisely to find the freedom from addictions we seek.

We engage in the relational aspect of forgiveness, making amends to all people we have hurt through our addictions, thoughts, words, and actions.

Compassionate action is an integral aspect of the path. We encourage you to find ways to be of service, to be generous, and to be kind. Once you maintain renunciation for over a year, establish a regular meditation practice, and complete the investigations, inventories, you are ready to become a mentor for others with your *Dharma Recovery*.

MINDFULNESS EXPERIENCE

BRINGING MINDFULNESS TO YOU

A group of people of diverse ages and cultural backgrounds sit in a circle together. Some are on chairs, and some sit on the floor. They are very still and quiet. It is almost as if they are breathing together like a single organism. What are they doing, or not doing? Everyone is in the silence of the circle. We radiate our good will: wishing well to ourselves, each other, the people around, our friends and families, and all living beings.

After thirty minutes a bell rings, eyes open, arms lift to stretch, and there are smiles as the people look around the room and catch each other's eyes. This is the true moment of the "Mindfulness Experience" – a Mindfulness Based Stress Reduction program which I conduct. These people have been on a journey together of transformation. I am grateful for all my fellow followers who participated in this program for our shared journey together. Everyone becomes their own and each other's teacher, as we practice this stillness and silence, called meditation. Even though I am the teacher, I am also being taught wisdom, kindness, and compassion by the fellow participants. We learned that relief from stress is possible and that we are all wise and whole. The capacity to be present in each moment is something that everyone has from the beginning. Now with this book as your guide, you can experience these teachings for yourself.

Mindfulness and compassionate practices will bring you a momentous shift in your life, something potentially huge and important, which just might transform your life with awareness and insight. You may discover that cultivating mindfulness and compassion has a way of giving you the understanding to reduce stress and suffering. Enjoy, the Ultimate Experience of Well-Being.

For the people who are too busy to meditate I recommend micro meditations. These are meditations that can be done several times a day for one to three minutes at a time. Periodically throughout the day, become aware of your breath. It could be when you feel yourself getting stressed or overwhelmed, with too much to do and too little time, or perhaps when you notice yourself becoming increasingly distracted and agitated. You will notice that by regularly practicing micro meditations you will become more aware and calm. You will find yourself becoming increasingly more mindful and focused. Micro meditations can put you back on track and help your mindfulness and compassionate muscle.

A second technique that can be used by the busy person is mindfulness in action, or compassion in action. Instead of adding a new routine to your day, just experience your day a little differently by paying attention in a mindful and compassionate way, for seconds at a time. With this practice you are training the mind to be right here, right now and opening your heart to others too.

Meditations from "Mindfulness Experience"

Awakening Awareness
Loving Kindness Meditation
Meditation on Compassion
Forgiveness Meditation
Gratitude Meditation
Body Scan Meditation
Mindfulness of the Body
Mindfulness of Feelings
Mindfulness of Mind States
Mindfulness of Mental Phenomena
Mindful Eating Meditation
Mindful Walking Meditation
Insight Meditations

NEW PLANET

"The new Planet will be blessed with love, compassion, peace, happiness and contentment finding solutions to violence, war, crime, poverty, energy, and environmental pollution through spirituality and science."

This book is itself is an awakening guide, a transformational tool, that has come out of the arising new consciousness. It is becoming clearer that there is less and less room for violent responses to fear and aggression. The sphere of our Green Planet has only so much room for more harmful weapons. Disrespect for our environment is a sign of diminished compassion. The world today is going through a transformation searching solutions for peace, poverty, and environmental pollution. As you read, a shift takes place within you. It can awaken those who are ready. Since many in the world are ready for it with each person who awakens, the momentum grows, and it becomes easier for others to follow creating a Green Planet Earth filled with love, compassion, peace, happiness, and contentment. An essential part of this awakening is the recognition of developing compassion to find a noble way to live. A new dimension of consciousness has begun to emerge on this planet. This new consciousness will create an awareness that will dissolve ego and the geographical boundaries that will search the Green Planet the peaceful oasis.

The Green Planet will be blessed with love, compassion, peace, happiness and contentment finding solutions to violence, war, crime, poverty, energy, and environmental pollution through science, spirituality and technological innovations. The existing limitations on food, wealth, and energy will overcome by mindful living, contentment, spirituality, science, technology, and innovation creating a peaceful Green Planet and human flourishing here on this Earth. The world needs the message in this book more than ever before to know compassionate solutions This understanding led me to writing this book out of my compassion.

We have an incredible capacity to wake up and move through hesitations and patterns of withdrawal to reach out to others and allow them to reach out to us through compassion. We have the ability to remember compassion as the genuine force of happiness and transformation that it is, no matter the world condition we face. We have the ability to face the ups and down of every day, to come to terms with the transience of life, and to reach for the grace and uplifting nature of compassion. May we celebrate the capacity each day of our precious lives by working to make this capacity a reality. Compassion can heal our lives – and transform our world, creating a Green Planet, the New Planet Earth.

Reflections on Compassion

*"May I mindfully meet
the suffering of others
with an open heart,
compassionately sharing with them
the emotions
natural to our human condition."*

"If you want to be happy, practice compassion."

"We cannot avert our eyes, looking around at those who suffer, those who are hungry, those who are ill or frightened. Our picture of life necessarily includes concern for everybody and everything including the environment."

"The compassion of the wise man does not render him a victim of suffering. His thoughts, words, and deeds are full of pity. But his heart does not waver; unchanged it remains, serene and calm. Compassion is a beautiful quality of the heart and intellect which knows, understands and is ready to help. Compassion that is strength and gives strength: this is the highest compassion. The highest manifestation of compassion is to show the world the path leading to the end of suffering."

"Most men have their eyes and ears closed to the suffering of others. They do not hear the cries of distress. They become deaf to their pleas and blind to their plight. They do not see the unbroken stream of tears flowing through life; they do not hear the cries of distress continually pervading the world. Bound by selfishness, their hearts turn stiff and narrow. Stiff and narrow, how should they be able to strive for any higher purpose? To realize that only the release of selfish cravings will affect their own freedom from suffering."

"Although we may win arguments, when we care only for ourselves, when we humiliate people and ignore their misery, it will almost always come back to us through the "Law of Karma." Therefore, if we want to be happy, it is essential to care for the welfare of others rather than categorizing some people as "enemies" whose needs are not important. We can instead care for their wellbeing. When we respect them as human beings and help them meet their basic needs, and their need to be respected, to give and receive care and affection, and to contribute to the welfare of a group, there will be no reason for them to be enemies. An enemy will become a friend."

"The foundation of compassion is when you come to perceive the real causes of suffering; the attachment to impermanence, delusional beliefs about the world, and selfish habits. When we see selfish, deluded people, we know that suffering is never far away. When we transcend our own self-centeredness and perceive the truth, compassion naturally follows."

"Dearest Friend, I sincerely wish you to be free from suffering and its causes. May your body be free from pain and your mind find contentment. I embrace you with my boundless compassion with no conditions. I truly care for you. Embrace the whole world with compassion."

- *Jayan E. Romesh*

May You be Free from
                    Suffering

    May You be Free from
                    Causes of Suffering

May All Beings be Free from
                    Suffering

    May All Beings be Free from
                    Causes of Suffering

About the Author

Jayan E. Romesh is an Engineer, Author, Speaker, and Spiritual Teacher. His books, writings, and teachings on Buddha Dharma, Mindfulness, Loving Kindness, Compassion, Forgiveness, Happiness, Enlightenment and various other insightful teachings have transformed many lives. His books, Happiness Now, Art of Loving Kindness, Path Less Traveled, Harmonious Way to Live, Seeds of Enlightenment, Boundless, Bliss and Beyond, and Each Moment A Joyful Moment, have enlightened his readers across the world. Jayan has attended workshops with the Insight Meditation Society in Vancouver, British Columbia, conducted by Adrianne Ross, Rachel Lewis, and Karen Lawrie. He has also completed Insight Meditation retreats under renowned meditation teachers, Michele McDonald, and Jesse Maceo Vega-Frey from Insight Meditation society in Barre, Massachusetts. Jayan follows workshops and programs conducted by Bestselling Authors, Dr. Rick Hanson, Eckhart Tolle, Jack Kornfield, Tara Brach and Pema Chodron. He is trained in Positive Neuroplasticity from Being Well, Inc. USA and Mindfulness Based Stress Reduction from Mindful Living, Vancouver, Canada. Jayan is the founder of *Metta Library* publishers, *"Jayan Innovations"* a Conscious Living initiative, *"Mindfulness Experience"*, a Mindfulness Based Stress Reduction (MBSR) program, *"Dharma Recovery"*, a Mindfulness Based Addiction Recovery (MBAR) Program, and the *Dharma Community* social media page that shares the wisdom teachings through *Dhamma Insights,* C-O-M-P-A-S-S-I-O-N and BOOKS FOR A CAUSE to help people in need. You will contribute to all of the above social services by purchasing the enlightening book, C-O-M-P-A-S-S-I-O-N. Born and raised in Sri Lanka, Jayan has learned and practiced Compassionate based teachings for over four decades. He migrated to Canada where he lives now.

Thank You for Reading
C-O-M-P-A-S-S-I-O-N

I really appreciate all of your feedback, and I love hearing what you have to say. I need your input to make the next version better. Please leave me a helpful review on Amazon letting me know what you thought of the book.

If you enjoyed the book, you'll want to visit www.mettalibrary.com where you can read many more! And while you're there, be sure to request free books, meditations, and join the email newsletter so you can be the first to read my latest writings, receive updates about when my next books will be available, receive guidance to write your own enlightening book, information about online training, and much more!

Thanks so much, with Love and Blessings,
 - Jayan E. Romesh

Books that Enlighten Lives
By Jayan E. Romesh
Available on Amazon Worldwide

Happiness Now

Path Less Traveled

Art of Loving Kindness

Harmonious Way to Live

SEEDS
OF
ENLIGHTENMENT

*Grow with Peace of Mind,
Boundless Love, and Lasting Happiness*

JAYAN E. ROMESH

Boundless, Bliss, and Beyond

Buddha's Sacred Teachings of
Opening the Heart and Stilling the Mind

Jayan E. Romesh

New From Metta Library

EACH MOMENT, A JOYFUL MOMENT

A Mindful Way to Greater Wisdom and Joy

Jayan E. Romesh

Metta Library

Books that Enlighten Lives
www.mettalibrary.com

Made in the USA
Monee, IL
05 June 2020